Traditional Chinese Sports

中国传统体育

○── 董华龙　主编

化学工业出版社

·北京·

《中国传统体育》依据《体育强国建设纲要》编写，旨在助力中国传统体育项目的国际化推广和发展。本书的主要内容由"健身气功五禽戏"和"24式简化太极拳"两部分组成，"健身气功五禽戏"是中国众多养生功法中最具代表性的功法之一，具有安全易学、左右对称的特点，养生价值极高。"24式简化太极拳"是众多中国武术门类中最具代表性的拳法之一，学习者有无基础均可习练，锻炼价值极高。

《中国传统体育》采用中英文对译方式编写，中文语言凝练，英文通俗易懂，书中通过文字和动作图片，详细介绍展示了两套功法的基本功、全套动作的练习方法，以及各动作要领和功效，方便读者形象直观地学习参考。本书附有数字资源，学习者扫描书中"二维码"，可观看19段动作学习高清视频（全部配有中英文字幕）。

《中国传统体育》可用作普通高校在华留学生的"体育与健康"课程的教材，亦可作为国内外广大体育爱好者学习、了解中国传统体育项目的兴趣读物。

图书在版编目（CIP）数据

中国传统体育＝Traditional Chinese Sports：汉英对照/董华龙主编．—北京：化学工业出版社，2020.7
ISBN 978-7-122-36497-5

Ⅰ.①中⋯ Ⅱ.①董⋯ Ⅲ.①民族形式体育-介绍-中国-汉、英 Ⅳ.①G852.9

中国版本图书馆CIP数据核字（2020）第047099号

责任编辑：刘心怡　　　　　　　　装帧设计：张　辉
责任校对：王　静

出版发行：化学工业出版社（北京市东城区青年湖南街13号　邮政编码100011）
印　　装：三河市延风印装有限公司
787mm×1092mm　1/16　印张8¾　字数247千字　2020年6月北京第1版第1次印刷

购书咨询：010-64518888　　　　　　售后服务：010-64518899
网　　址：http://www.cip.com.cn
凡购买本书，如有缺损质量问题，本社销售中心负责调换。

定　价：36.00元　　　　　　　　　　　　　　　　　　版权所有　违者必究

前 言
Preface

2019 年 8 月，国务院办公厅发布《体育强国建设纲要》(《纲要》)，《纲要》明确指出：为提升中国体育国际影响力，实施中华武术"走出去"战略，推动中国传统体育项目的国际化发展。近年来，兰州石化职业技术学院以建设有特色高水平高职院校为目标，按照"地方离不开、行业都认同、国际能交流"的教学原则，积极响应"一带一路"倡议，为"一带一路"沿线国家培养当地需要的技术人才。自 2017 年 10 月学校迎来首批留学生至今，学校已有来自巴基斯坦、老挝、吉尔吉斯斯坦、哈萨克斯坦、文莱、印度尼西亚、塔吉克斯坦和索马里兰等多国留学生。体育作为"无国界"的交流项目非常受青年人喜爱，特别是中国传统体育项目备受青睐。在高级别人文交流机制的示范和引领下，体育活动有力增进了各国人民间的友谊和文明互鉴；站在人文交流事业全面发展的新时代，需要秉持人文交流理念，强化人文交流意识，提升人文交流的能力和素养，更好地发挥中国传统体育在中外文化教育交流中的作用。

In August 2019, the General Office of the State Council issued *Construction Outline of Sports Strengthening China*. The outline explicitly points out that in order to improve the international influence of Chinese sports, the going-out strategy of Chinese Wushu is to be put into effect to promote the international development of Chinese traditional sports events. In recent years, our college (Lan zhou Petrochemical College of Vocational Technology) has set up the construction of a characteristic and high-level vocational college as the goal to reach the purpose that the local cannot leave, all the industries approve, and international communication can be made, and to cultivate the local talents in the "Belt and Road" countries to response the "Belt and Road" intiative. Since October 2017, when our college ushered in the 1st batch of international students, there are many international students on the campus from Pakistan, Laos, Kyrgyzstan, Kazakhstan, Brunei, Indonesia, Tajikistan, and Somaliland. Sports as a "non-boundary" communicative event, is very popular among the youth, especially the Chinese traditional sports among international students. Under the guidance of high-grade humanity communication mechanism, sports promote the friendship and civilization communication among countries. During the new era of the integrated cultural and educational exchange development, the concept of the cultural and educational exchange needs adhering to the consciousness of the cultural and educational exchange enhancing, and the ability and quality of the cultural and educational exchange improving, thus the role of the Chinese traditional sports in the cultural and educational exchange will be developed better.

《中国传统体育》一书基本内容由"健身气功五禽戏"和"24式简化太极拳"两部分组成,"健身气功五禽戏"是中国众多养生功法中最具代表性的功法之一,主要以模仿虎、鹿、熊、猿、鸟动作为主,具有安全易学、左右对称的特点,养生价值极高。"24式简化太极拳"是众多中国武术门类中最具代表性的拳法之一,学习者有无基础均可练习,锻炼价值极高。

为提高留学生的学习能力和交流能力,本书在编写时突出以下特点:

1. 双语教学

教材全文采用中英文对译方式,中文语言凝练,英文通俗易懂,便于留学生独立学习。

2. 理实均衡

全书由两部分组成,每部分三章,两章理论,一章实践,理论与实践篇幅均等,理论学习有利于了解中国传统文化,实践学习有利于掌握传统技法。

3. 图文并茂

利用体育直观性特点,书中实践部分采用260多幅动作图片,详细地描述了两套功法的基本功和套路动作,便于留学生直观学习。

4. 高清视频、双语字幕

教材采用了"融合教材"编写模式,将纸质教材与数字资源内容相结合,学习者扫描书中"二维码",可获得19段动作学习高清视频(全部配有中英文字幕)等教材相关的富媒体资源。

The book, *Chinese Traditional Sports*, comprises 2 parts: Fitness Qigong and Five-animal Exercise, 24-form Simplified Tai Chi Boxing. Fitness Qigong and Five-animal Exercise is one of the most representative fitness and health methods, which mainly imitates the actions of animals like tigers, deer, bears, apes, and birds, and whose actions are symmetric and easy for learning. 24-form Simplified Tai Chi Boxing one of the most representative boxing methods in various Chinese Wushu types, which is worthwhile playing, and can be learned by beginners without foundation.

The book has the following features while being composed to improve students' learning and communication ability.

1. Bilingual education

The whole book is edited in Chinese and English, Chinese being compact and concise, English popular and easy for international students to understand and learn independently.

2. Balanced theoretical and practical education

The book consists of 2 parts, each of which comprises 2 chapters of theory and 1 chapter of practice, both of which are the same length. The theory study helps to comprehend Chinese traditional culture, and the practice aids in mastering the traditional exercise methods.

3. Excellent essays accompanied by nice pictures

With the sport's characteristic of intuition, the practice part of the book adopts 268 action diagrams, describing the basic methods and actions in details, for the international students to learn intuitively.

4. High-definition videos, bilingual subtitles

The book adopts the integrated-textbook editing mode, integrating the paper text-book with the digital material. When the learners scan the QR code, they can obtain the text-book related rich-media resources—19 HD videos with Chinese and English subtitles to learn.

本书由董华龙任主编并负责统稿，杨喜存负责英语翻译，王谦、陈兴廷参与编写。具体分工为：董华龙编写第一章、第二章、第三章、第四章第一节、第五章、第六章中文部分，并负责全书的图片拍摄和视频录制；王谦、陈兴廷编写第四章第二节中文部分；杨喜存编写第一章、第二章、第三章、第四章、第五章、第六章英语部分。

中国传统体育是一个古老而又新兴的学科，系统研究尚处在不断探索过程之中，加之编者水平有限，书中不免存在一些欠缺和不足，敬请广大读者和关心中国传统体育的同仁批评指正。

The book is edited and finalized by Dong Hualong, English version responsible by Yang Xicun, co-edited by Wang Qian and Chen Xingting. The concrete division is that: Dong Hualong edited Chapter Ⅰ, Ⅱ, Ⅲ, Section I in chapter Ⅳ, and Chinese versions in Chapter Ⅴ and Ⅵ, and all the diagrams and videos. Wang Qian and Chen Xingting finished the Chinese version in section Ⅱ of Chapter Ⅳ.

Since Chinese traditional sports is an old and emerging academic discipline, a systematic study on it is still on the way, and with the limited knowledge of the editor, thus more of fewer deficiencies exist in the book. So welcome sincerely the criticisms from readers and colleagugs concerning the Chinese traditional sports.

董华龙
2019 年 10 月

Dong Hualong
October, 2019

目 录
CONTENTS

第一章　健身气功概述　/ 1	
第一节　健身气功的概念	1
第二节　健身气功的特点	4
第三节　健身气功的价值	5
第四节　健身气功的练习要素	8

第二章　健身气功·五禽戏概述　/ 25	
第一节　功法起源	25
第二节　功法特点	26
第三节　习练要领	27

第三章　健身气功·五禽戏动作图解　/ 29	
第一节　基本功	29
第二节　动作图解	32

第四章　太极拳概述　/ 69	
第一节　太极拳简史	69
第二节　武德与武礼	73

第五章　太极拳技术分析及训练方法　/ 75	
第一节　太极拳的运动风格	75
第二节　太极拳的技术分析	76
第三节　太极拳的训练方法	79

第六章　24式太极拳动作图解　/ 83	
第一节　基本功	83
第二节　动作图解	86

参考文献　/ 134

Chapter 1　Summary of Fitness Qigong　/ 1	
Section 1　The concept of Fitness Qigong	1
Section 2　Characteristics of Fitness Qigong	4
Section 3　The Value of Fitness Qigong	5
Section 4　Exercise Elements of Fitness Qigong	8

Chapter 2　Summary of Fitness Qigong · Wu Qin Xi　/ 25	
Section 1　Origin and Development of Exercise Methods	25
Section 2　Features of Exercise Methods	26
Section 3　Main Exercise Methods	27

Chapter 3　The Movement Illustration of Fitness Qigong · Wu Qin Xi　/ 29	
Section 1　Basic Techniques	29
Section 2　Illustration of Movement	32

Chapter 4　Summary of Taiji Quan　/ 69	
Section 1　A Brief History of Taiji Quan	69
Section 2　Martial Moralities and Manners	73

Chapter 5　Technical Analysis on and Training Methods of Taiji Quan　/ 75	
Section 1　Sports Style of Taiji Quan	75
Section 2　Technical Analysis of Taiji Quan	76
Section 3　Training Methods of Taiji Quan	79

Chapter 6　The Movement Illustration of Twenty-four Style Taiji Quan　/ 83	
Section 1　Basic Techniques	83
Section 2　Illustration of Movement	86

References　/ 134

第一章　健身气功概述
Chapter 1　Summary of Fitness Qigong

本章要点：健身气功作为中华民族传统体育项目，具有鲜明的时代特征和广泛的群众基础，在全民健身活动中、在对外文化交流中均发挥着不可替代的作用。本章主要讲述健身气功的概念及其涵义，并对健身气功的健身特点、时代价值和练习要素进行了阐述。

Key points：Fitness Qigong, as a traditional sports event of China, has distinct characteristics of the times and a broad mass foundation. It plays an irreplaceable role in national fitness activities and cultural exchanges with foreign countries. This chapter mainly describes the concept and meaning of fitness Qigong, and expounds the fitness characteristics, times value and exercise elements of fitness Qigong.

第一节　健身气功的概念

Section 1　The concept of Fitness Qigong

气功是中华民族的瑰宝，具有悠久的历史和深厚的文化底蕴。它作为一种独特的身心锻炼方法，在中国养生学中占据着十分重要的地位。气功是"吐纳""导引""按跷""行气"等传统健身方法的代名词。气功一词最初见于晋代许逊所著的《灵剑子》，直到20世纪50年代《气功疗法实践》和《内养功疗法》问世后，才被人们广泛使用。但究竟什么叫气功，不了解气功或初学气功的人会感到神秘，而研究气功的人往往从不同的视角出发，各有所见，莫衷一是。有人认为气功的"气"就是呼吸之气，将气功译成 Breathing Exercise，即呼吸操；有人把气功看作是一种特别适用于老弱病人的医疗保健方法，等等。如果从健身养生的视角出发，普遍比较认同的气功内涵是：气功是基于中华传统文化的人体生命整体观，通过调

Qigong is the treasure of the Chinese nation, with a long history and profound cultural heritage. As a unique physical and psychological exercise method, it occupies a very important position in Chinese health science. Qigong is synonymous with traditional fitness methods such as "Expiration & Inspiration", "Guiding", "acting on stilts", "Circulation of Qi" and so on. The expression of Qigong was first appeared in the book "*Lin Jianzi*" written by Xu Xun in Jin Dynasty and was not widely used until the 1950s when *Qigong Therapy Practice* and *Breathing Exercise Therapy* were published. But for the people who don't know Qigong or learn Qigong, Qigong is mysterious, and Qigong researchers often start from different perspectives and have their views. Some people think Qigong's "Qi" is the breath of air, which is translated as Breathing Exercise, some people regard Qigong as a health care method especially suitable for old and weak patients, and so on. For fitness, Qigong is generally agreed that Qigong is a holistic view of human life based

心、调息、调身的锻炼，改善自身的健康状况，开发人体潜能，使身心高度和谐的技能。

20 世纪 80 年代，气功在社会上一度风行，为使社会气功步入科学化、规范化、法制化管理的轨道，保证气功活动健康有序地发展，中共中央宣传部、原国家体育运动委员会（国家体委）和原卫生部等七个部委于 1996 年 8 月联合下发了《关于加强社会气功管理的通知》，第一次提出了什么是社会气功，什么是健身气功，什么是气功医疗："社会气功是指社会上众多人员参与的健身气功和气功医疗活动""群众通过参加锻炼，从而强身健体、养生康复的，属于健身气功""对他人传授或运用气功疗法直接治疗疾病，构成医疗行为的，属气功医疗"。

2000 年 9 月，国家体育总局颁布的《健身气功管理暂行办法》，对健身气功概念作了进一步的界定，指出"健身气功是以自身形体活动、呼吸吐纳、心理调节相结合为主要运动形式的民族传统体育项目，是中华悠久文化的组成部分"。2006 年 11 月，国家体育总局颁布的《健身气功管理办法》，继续沿用了这一概念。

体育是以身体练习为基本手段，以增强体质、促进人的全面发展、丰富社

on Chinese traditional culture, and that Qigong can improve one's health and develop its human potential by adjusting heart, interest, and body by improving one's health condition and developing the potential of the human body, the Qigong is based on the traditional Chinese culture and is a skill that connects the mind and body with a high degree of harmony.

In the 1980s, Qigong was once popular in society. In August 1996, in order to bring social Qigong into the track of scientific, standardized and legalized management, and to ensure the healthy and orderly development of Qigong activities, seven ministries such as the Propaganda Ministry of the CPC Central Committee, the State Sports Commission and the Ministry of Health, jointly issued *the Notice on strengthening the Management of Social Qigong*, which for the first time put forward what Social Qigong is, what physical Qigong is, and what Qigong Medical treatment is. Social Qigong refers to the fitness Qigong and Qigong medical activities in which many people participate in the society; Fitness Qigong is such an exercise the masses who take part in to strengthen their physical fitness and restore their health; Qigong Medical Treatment is a kind of medical treatment if Qigong therapy is taught or applied to others directly to treat diseases, which involves medical behavior.

In September 2000, *the Interim Measures for the Administration of Fitness Qigong* issued by the State Administration of Physical Education further defined the concept of Fitness Qigong and pointed out that "Fitness Qigong is one of traditionally national sports, and part of Chinese long-history culture, which is a combined practice of breathing and toning with one's own physique, and psychological adjustments as the main form of sports." In November 2006, the "Fitness Qigong Management Method" issued by the State Administration of physical Education continued to follow this concept.

Sport is a kind of conscious and organized social activity aimed at strengthening physique, promoting the all-round development of human beings, enriching social

会文化生活和促进精神文明为目的的一种有意识、有组织的社会活动。体育是通过身体运动的方式进行的，它要求人体直接参与活动，这是体育最本质的特点之一，这一特点决定了体育具有健身功能。健身气功同样以自我身体锻炼为基本手段，同样要求直接参与活动，同样具有健身功能。健身气功锻炼的强身健体功能，不仅包含着形体的健康，还包含着心理健康；健身气功锻炼的养生康复功能，不仅能够预防疾病，还能够祛病健身、延年益寿。因此，健身气功是一种体育项目，充分体现了自我锻炼的健身特征。

历史上对气功也有多种分类，如按历史源流分为道家气功、儒家气功、释家气功、医家气功、武术气功；按练功的状态分为动功、静功；按功法姿势分为站功、坐功、卧功、行功。历史上对气功的分类情形十分复杂，实际上同一类气功也有很多流派，同一流派又有很多支派。在新的历史时期，将社会气功分为健身气功和医疗气功，不仅适应了对社会气功管理的需要，而且也符合气功发展的客观规律。气功历经数千年发展到今天，不仅有着广泛的群众基础，而且成为全民健身的一种重要锻炼方法。将以自我锻炼为主要形式，以强身健体、养生康复为目的的气功划为健身气功，将由医者向患者实施以治疗疾病为目的的气功划为医疗气功，更有利于气功学科领域的建设，更有利于气功事业的发展。随着"一带一路"交流的日益频繁，健身气功作为一个重要的文化载体，将成为沿线国家人民的共同财富。

and cultural life and promoting spiritual civilization by taking physical exercise as the basic means. Sports is carried out through the way of physical exercise, which requires the human body to directly participate in the activities, which is one of the most essential features of sports, which determines that sports have the function of fitness. Fitness Qigong also takes self-physical exercise as the basic means, requires direct participation in activities, and has fitness function. The physical function of Qigong exercise enhances not only the health of the body, but also mental health. Its health rehabilitation function, not only can prevent disease, but also can dispel disease and keep fit, and aids in prolonging life. Therefore, the Fitness Qigong belongs to the sports, fully reflects the fitness characteristics of self-exercise.

There are many kinds of Qigong in history. It can be classified as Taoism Qigong, Confucian Qigong, Buddhism Qigong, Medical Qigong, Wushu Qigong according to its historical origins; be divided into Dynamic Qigong and Static Qigong according to the practicing status; and standing Qigong, sitting Qigong, lying Qigong, walking Qigong according to the practice postures. The classification of Qigong in history is very complicated. In fact, there are many schools and branches of the same kind of Qigong. In the new historical period, the division of Social Qigong into Fitness Qigong and Medical Qigong not only meets the needs of Social Qigong management, but also accords with the objective law of Qigong development. After thousands of years of development, Qigong has a wide range of people basic, and become an important exercise method of national fitness. Qigong, which takes self-exercise as the main form, is classified as Qigong for the purpose of strengthening physical fitness and health-preserving and rehabilitating, and as medical Qigong for the purpose of treating diseases by doctors, which is more conducive to the construction of Qigong discipline, and more conducive to the development of Qigong development. With the increasingly frequent exchanges along the Belt and Road, Fitness Qigong, as an important cultural carrier, will become the commonwealth of the people of the countries along the route.

第二节　健身气功的特点

健身气功是以自身形体活动，呼吸吐纳，心理调节相结合为主要运动形式的民族传统体育项目。它与其他体育锻炼相比，有其鲜明的健身特点。

一、注重整体锻炼

人的生命是精神与肉体的统一，人与一般动物的根本区别在于具有特有的意识活动。如果从外形、气息、精神三位一体的人体生命整体观出发，健身气功调身、调息、调心的综合锻炼，正是区别于其他肢体运动锻炼的关键所在。显现肢体外部运动的体育锻炼，并不注重意和气的运用。而健身气功锻炼的特性就在于其主动地、内向性地运用意识，通过调整人体内在潜力，从而改善和增进人的整体功能，达到强身健体的目的。

二、运动风格绵缓

柔和绵缓是健身气功运动的一个显著特征。它不仅表现在肢体外形和动作演练上不拘不僵、轻松自如、舒展大方、轻飘徐缓，而且在呼吸调控上也应做到深、细、匀、长，就是在意念的运用上也要求精神放松、意识平静、用意要轻、似有似无。这种动作圆滑、心意慢运的行功节奏，体现了低强度、长时间下的运动特点，可避免大强度运动后给人体生理带来的各种负效应，有利于在节能的情况下均匀地提高机体的各种生理功能。由于健身气功锻炼柔缓绵长，沉着稳定，单位时间的负荷不大，所以任何人群均可习练。

Section 2　Characteristics of Fitness Qigong

Fitness Qigong is a traditional national sports event, which combines physical activity, breathing and psychological adjustment as the main form of sports. Compared with other physical exercises, it has its distinctive fitness characteristics.

1. Focus on the overall exercise

Human life is the unity of spirit and body. The fundamental difference between human and ordinary animals lies in their unique conscious activities. With the point view of the human body trinity of the appearance, breath, and spirit, the comprehensive exercise of adjusting the body, the breath, and the heart in Fitness Qigong is the key point different from other physical exercises. Physical exercises that show physical activity outside the limbs do not focus on the use of breathing. The character of Fitness Qigong exercise lies in its positive, inner use with consciousness, by adjusting the inner potential of the human body, thereby improving and promoting the overall function of the human body, to achieve the purpose of strengthening the body.

2. Gentle sports style

Being gentle and slow is a remarkable feature of Qigong exercise. It is not only manifested in the appearance of the limbs and in the exercise of movement, relaxing, gentle and slow, but also in respiratory regulation and control, it should also be deep, thin, even, long, even in the use of the mind it also requires spiritual relaxation. Consciousness is calm, intended to be light as if there was nothing. This kind of movement is round and the rhythm of slow movement reflects the characteristics of low intensity and long-time threshold, which can avoid all kinds of negative effects on human physiology after high-intensity exercise. It is beneficial to improve the physiological function of the body evenly under the condition of saving energy. Because of fitness Qigong exercise being gentle and long, calm and stable, and no

三、养生作用明显

养生，又称摄生，就是"治未病"。人的身体素质如何，疾病的发生与否，主要取决于人体机能的状况。从一定意义上讲，健身气功就是改善人体机能的运动，例如，人的情绪波动属于心理反应，一般情况下并不足以致病，但超过心理活动调节的范围，就会引起体内阴阳、气血、脏腑的功能失调而发生疾病。健身气功锻炼时，强调放松机体、平衡呼吸、安静大脑，它可直接作用于中枢神经及自主神经系统，缓冲不良情绪对大脑的刺激，降低大脑的应急性反应，从而维持人体内环境的相对稳定，即可达到抵御外邪、祛病强身的目的。

第三节 健身气功的价值

健身气功这一概念的提出，既是对传统气功的继承，又适应了时代发展的要求。它不仅反映了传统气功在中华文化中的重要地位和作用，也指明了传统气功的发展方向，具有重要的历史意义和现实意义。

一、健身气功的社会价值

构建社会主义和谐社会是一项系统工程，需要社会方方面面的共同努力。健身气功锻炼追求身心的和谐，注重从人自身的和谐进入到人与社会的和谐、人与自然的和谐，从某种意义上讲，健身气功是一门关于"和谐"的学问。健身气功"天人合一"的理论基础，以及三合一的练功方法，就充分体现了深刻

large load in the unit time, any group can practice.

3. Obvious effect of health preservation

Health preservation, also known as ingestion, is to "prevent the disease in advance". People's physical quality, the occurrence of disease, mainly depends on the conditions of the human body function. In a certain sense, Fitness Qigong is the exercise to improve the function of the human body. For example, people's emotional fluctuations belong to psychological reactions, and in general, they are not enough to cause disease, but beyond the scope of regulation of psychological activities, they will cause the dysfunction of Yin and Yang, qi, blood and viscera in the body, thus cause diseases. When exercising Fitness Qigong, emphasis should be placed on relaxing the body, balancing breathing and calming the brain. It can directly act on the central nervous system and the vegetative nervous system, buffer the stimulation of bad emotions to the brain, and reduce the response of the brain, thus to maintain the comparative stability of the inner circumstance of the body, which can achieve the purpose of resisting external evil, eliminating disease and strengthening the body.

Section 3　The Value of Fitness Qigong

The concept of Fitness Qigong not only inherits the traditional Qigong, but also adapts to the development of the times. It reflects the important position and function of traditional Qigong in Chinese culture, and points out the development direction of traditional Qigong, which has important historical and practical significance.

1. The social value of fitness qigong

Building a harmonious socialist society is a systematic project, which requires the joint efforts of all aspects of society. Fitness Qigong pursues the harmony of body and mind, pays attention to the harmony between human beings and society, and the harmony between man and nature. In a sense, Fitness Qigong is knowledge of "harmony". The theoretical basis of Fitness Qigong's "unity of nature and man" and the

的"和谐"思想内涵。实践表明,人们在进行健身气功锻炼的同时,还渗透着道德涵养的修炼和提升。因此,无论是从增强人民体质而言,还是从建设社会主义精神文明而言,推广普及健身气功是一项功在当代、利在千秋的事业,同样是在为构建和谐社会作贡献。

method of practicing "harmony" fully embody the profound thought of "harmony". Practice shows that people in the exercise of Fitness Qigong, permeate moral training and promotion. So, whether in terms of improving the people's health, or in the construction of socialist spiritual civilization, popularizing Qigong is a contemporary and beneficial career, and is also contributing to the construction of a harmonious society.

二、健身气功的文化价值

健身气功是中国传统文化的产物,是中国传统文化沉积的反应。因此,健身气功在理论上受传统文化的思想指导,在行为方式上受传统文化的制约。健身气功植根于中国的文化土壤,犹如一棵枝叶茂盛的大树,其根须伸展到四面八方,吸收着各方面的养分,其文化理论渊源是多元的,它既吸收了中国传统哲学思想和文化理念,又蕴含了医学、美学等传统科学的内核。

健身气功是具有中国风格的技艺。中华气功从古至今的发展,在内部结构和外部形态上既有"形"与"神"的交融,也渗透着民族的风格、习惯、心理、感情等因素。可以说,中国人独特的思维方式、行为规范、审美观念、心态模式、价值取向和人生观等在健身气功中都有不同的反映。比如其"德"与"艺"的统一、淡漠的竞争意识,注重个人技艺的纯熟,富于观赏而追求高尚的精神气质等,与西方文明所突出的壮烈、惊险,富于强烈刺激性的审美观形成鲜明的对照。健身气功交织着阴阳二气组合的生命律动,外取神态,内表心灵,着重在姿态的意境里显示人格,堪称传统体育文化的代表。

2. The cultural value of fitness qigong

Fitness Qigong is the product of Chinese traditional culture and reflects the deposit of Chinese traditional culture. Therefore, it is guided by the traditional culture in theory and restricted by the traditional culture in the way of behavior. Fitness Qigong is rooted in the cultural soil of China, just like a big tree with lush branches and leaves, and its roots extending in all directions, absorbing nutrients from all aspects. Its cultural and theoretical origins are diverse. It not only absorbs the traditional Chinese philosophy and cultural ideas, but also contains the core of traditional science such as medicine and aesthetics.

Fitness Qigong is art with Chinese style. With the development of Qigong from ancient times to the present, the "spirit" in the internal structure and "shape" in the external form of Qigong not only blend together, but also permeate the national style, habit, psychology, emotion and so on. It can be said that Chinese people's unique way of thinking, behavior norms, aesthetic concepts, mental mode, value orientation and outlook on life have been reflected through Fitness Qigong in various ways. For example, its unity of "virtue" and "art", indifferent sense of competition, focus on the pure skill of the individuals, the spiritual temperament in appreciation and pursuit of nobleness, has a sharp contrast with the Western aesthetics which highlights brave, strength, adventures, and strong stimulation. Fitness Qigong is intertwined with the life rhythm of the combination of Yin and Yang. It can be regarded as the representative of traditional sports culture, because of external expression, inner expression of the soul, and emphasis on the expression of personality in the mood of posture.

综上所述，习练健身气功既是为了强身健体，也是为了领悟和弘扬传统文化，还可以使人懂得"做人的真谛"而"完善人生的价值"。由此可见，深刻认识健身气功文化的现实价值，深入挖掘健身气功文化中的积极成分，汲取健身气功文化合理的思想内核，使之与现代科学相适应，与当今文明相协调，同样是建设先进文化不可或缺的内容。

三、健身气功的体育价值

随着物质生活水平的不断提高，闲暇时间的增多，人们的体育健身意识不断增强，参与体育活动的人数也逐步增多。体育不仅成为了身体锻炼的重要方式，而且成为了社会时尚的代名词。"少吃药，多流汗""花钱买健康"已为人们所共识，并有越来越多的人参加到体育锻炼中来。由于健身气功不仅健身作用明显，而且内容丰富，形式多样，不同的功法有着不同的动作结构、风格特点和运动量，并且不受年龄、性别、体质、时间、季节、场地、器械等限制，人们可以根据自己的需要和条件，选择合适的功法进行锻炼。因此，作为民族传统体育项目的健身气功，在满足人民群众多元化的健身需求，推动全民健身活动蓬勃发展中发挥着重要作用。

随着"一带一路"（the Belt and Road）的深入推进，沿线各国的交流日益频繁，健身气功作为中国传统文化的重要组成部分，在各国之间的文化交流、体育交流活动中也逐渐发挥出重要的作用。

To sum up, the practice of Qigong is not only to strengthen physical fitness, but also to help understand and promote traditional culture, make people understand "the true meaning of being a person" and "perfect the value of life". It can also be seen from this that a deep understanding of the practical value of the Fitness Qigong culture, in-depth excavation of the positive elements of the culture of Fitness Qigong, drawing on the rational ideological core of the culture of Fitness Qigong, so as to adapt it to modern science, and to coordinate with today's civilization, is an indispensable part of building an advanced culture.

3. The sports value of fitness qigong

With the continuous improvement of the living standard, the increase of leisure time, and people's enhanced consciousness of physical fitness, the number of people involved in sports activities is gradually increasing. Sports, synonymous with social fashion, has become an important way of physical exercise. "Less medicine, more sweat", "paying money for health" have been recognized and accepted, and more people take part in physical exercises. Fitness Qigong has obvious fitness function, and rich content and various forms. Its techniques have different movement structures, style characteristics, and exercise quantity, and its practice is not affected by ages, sexes, physique, time, seasons, venues, equipments and so on. Thus, people can choose the right exercise according to their own needs and conditions. Therefore Fitness Qigong, as a traditional national sports event, plays an important role in meeting the diverse needs of the people and promoting the vigorous development of national fitness activities.

With the in-depth advancement of the "Belt and Road" initiative, exchanges among countries along the route have become increasingly frequent. As an important part of Chinese traditional culture, Fitness Qigong is a cultural exchange among countries. Sports exchange activities also gradually play an important role.

第四节　健身气功的练习要素

调身、调息、调心是健身气功锻炼的三个基本要素。

第一要素：调身

调身是初学气功者入门的阶梯，是健身气功的重要内容。所谓调身，是指练功者对基本身形和肢体运动的调控，使之符合练功量度的要求，又称为身形合度。调身主要是通过筋、膜、骨、肉之间合理的相对运动来实现的。

一、调身的作用

健身气功不是短时间内身体的激烈运动，而是以特定的动作，循序渐进地调整人体的生理功能。通过习练健身气功功法，带动四肢乃至全身关节骨骼，进而牵动内脏器官运动，逐渐提高全身肢体关节、韧带、骨骼的灵活性和协调性，从而起到柔筋健骨、疏通经络、调畅气血的作用。调身是通过形体运动与精神、意识、气息活动的适当配合使之彼此促进，正确引动形体可以起到人静养神的作用。古人云："形不正则气不顺，气不顺则意不宁，意不宁则神散乱。"由此可见，调身是调息和调心的基础。

二、调身的方法

人的姿态虽然千变万化，但不外乎行、立、坐、卧四个基本姿势，古人称为"四威仪"。所谓"立如松，坐如钟，

Section 4　Exercise Elements of Fitness Qigong

Physical adjustment, breathing adjustment, and psychological adjustment are the three basic elements of Qigong exercise.

Element 1　Physical Adjustment

Physical adjustment as the beginning step for Qigong beginners, and an important part of Fitness Qigong, also known as the fitness of the body and figure, refers to the adjustment and control of the basic body figure and the limb movements by the practitioners, to meet the requirements of the exercise amount. Physical adjustment is mainly achieved through reasonable and relative joint movements of tendon, membrane, bone, and muscle.

1. The effect of physical adjustment

Fitness Qigong is not the intense physical exercise in a short period, but a specific action to adjust the physiological function of the human body gradually. By practicing the Fitness Qigong, the limbs and even all the bones of the joints of the extremities are put in motion, and then drive the movements of the internal organs, gradually to improve the flexibility and coordination of the joints, ligaments, and bones of the limbs throughout the body, so as to reach the effect of softening the tendon, strengthening the bones, dredging the meridians and collaterals, and regulating qi and blood circulation. Physical adjustment is fulfilled through the proper coordination of physical movement, spirit, consciousness, and breath activities to promote each other. The correct movement of the body can make people calm and the spirit improved. The ancients said: "if the shape is not regular, the breath will not be smooth, and if the breath is not smooth, the mind will be restless. Then the spirit is scattered." It can be seen that physical adjustment is the basis of breathing adjustment and psychological adjustment.

2. The way to adjust

Although the human posture is ever-changing, it is nothing more than walking, standing, sitting, lying in the four basic positions, which is called the "four

卧如弓，行如风"，以及屈伸俯仰、升降开合、转摇跑跳，这些都是历史上调身的具体方法。本节重点介绍以下几种方法。

dignities." in the ancient time. The old saying "standing like a pine, sitting like a bell, lying like a bow, walking like the wind", as well as bending and stretching, leaning and raising, lifting and falling, opening and closing, turning and swinging, running and jumping, are the specific methods of historical adjustment. This section focuses on the following methods.

(1) 自然势

两脚平行站立，与肩同宽，头正颈直，百会虚领，下颌微收，舌尖平放，唇齿相合，沉肩坠肘，腋下虚掩，含胸拔背，腰腹放松，两膝微屈，两手自然垂于体侧，目平视前方。

(1) Natural gesture

Standing with the feet in parallel, with the width of shoulders, head and neck straight, Baihui temple virtually leading, the chin backwards a little, tongue tip flat, lip and tooth matching, shoulder and elbows lower, armpit open a little, chest backward and back bent, waist and abdomen relaxed, two knees slightly bent, both hands naturally hanging to the body sides, eyes looking straight forward.

(2) 抱球势

在自然势的状态下，两臂先内旋摆至体侧，再变外旋，两掌向前环抱于胸前与胸部同高，指尖相对间距约10厘米，同时松腰沉裆，屈膝收髋敛臀，上体保持中正，目平视前方。此势也可两掌抱于腹前与脐同高。

(2) Ball holding gesture

In the state of natural gesture, the 2 arms were swung to the side of the body first, then turned outward, the two hands were folded forward in front of the chest at the same height of the breast, the relative distance between the fingertips was about 10 cm, and at the same time loosen the waist and sank the crotch, bend the knee and retract the hip and converge the hip, the upper body maintain straight, and look forward straight. This gesture can also be that both hands held in front of the abdomen and at the belly button height.

(3) 扶按势

在自然势的状态下，坐腕舒指，两臂内旋前伸，与肩同宽，高与胸平，随之屈肘两掌下按腹前或髋旁，其余要求与抱球势相同。

(3) Support gesture

In the state of natural gesture, keep the wrist relaxed and fingers straight, and make the arms rotate inside and stretch forward with the width of the shoulders, reach the height of the chest, then bend the elbow and press downwards in front of the abdomen or the hip sides, the other requirements are the same as in Ball Holding Gesture.

(4) 叠掌势

在自然势的状态下，两臂先内旋再外旋经体侧两掌向前环抱，随之回收两掌叠于腹前，掌心对准肚脐或脐下。

(4) Overlapping gesture

In the state of natural gesture, the arms first rotate inside and then outside, the two palms encircle forward, and then the two palms are folded in front of the abdomen, and the palms are centered on the navel or under the navel.

三、调身的要求

3. Adjustment requirements

调身如何引动形体，因功法、姿势、动作的不同而异，其基本要求为：

How the body adjustment motivates the shape varies a lot due to different function methods, postures, and movements. The basic requirements are as follows:

（1）引动形体要运用意识

(1) The consciousness motivating the body

运用意识来引动形体，主要是先使意识与形体相合，要求姿势正确，在正确姿势的导引下，促使气血流转，从而达到周身气血畅通。

Using consciousness to motivate the body is mainly to make the consciousness fit with the body, requiring the correct postures, under the guidance of which the circulation of Qi and blood is promoted, so as to achieve the smooth flow of Qi and blood through the whole body.

（2）形体放松，动作柔软

(2) Relaxed bodies, and soft movements

形体放松，但要松而不懈；动作柔软，但要柔而不软。动作要用意不用力，即不用拙力，这样才能通体柔和，气血畅达。

Bodies are relaxed, but not sluggish; movements are soft, but not weak. Consciousness instead of force. Brute force is used to drive movements, thus the body can be soft, and Qi and blood smooth and fluent.

（3）动势圆活

(3) Smooth movements

每一个姿势，周身上下均要避免出现死角，处处要有圆撑之意。动起来要圆而灵活，不以刚直为用，而有螺旋或抽丝（又称缠丝）之意。

Every pose of the whole body, avoiding dead ends, moves smoothly and fluently everywhere. The movements should be smooth and flexible, not rigid, like rotating spirals or wrapping wires.

（4）动作连绵不断

(4) Continuous movements

动作要快慢适度，快而不停，慢而不断，达到动作断气息不断，气息断意识不断的状态。

The speed of movements should moderate, neither fast nor slow without stops, and the Qi remains continuous even when the movements pause, and the consciousness remains continuous even when the Qi rests.

（5）腰为主宰

(5) Waist is dominant

有两层含义：一是腰部放松是全身放松的关键；二是做动作时应以腰主导一身的活动，即"力发于足，主宰于腰，形于四肢"。

There are two meanings: first, the relaxation of the waist is the key to the relaxation of the whole body; the other is the movements should be dominated by the waist, that is, "strength from the foot, control from the waist, and shapes from the limbs".

（6）分清虚实

(6) Distinguish between real or virtual movements

这是练功保持周身中正的关键。人

This is the key to practice and maintain the integrity

of the whole body. In order to maintain the balance of the body, the change law of the every real and the virtual movement must be carefully understood and grasped since the center of gravity of the human body changes with the change of posture.

(7) *Integrated ups and downs*

In practice, one must pay attention to the whole body. Although the requests for practicing Qigong is not as strict with the hands, eyes, body style and steps as in martial arts, it requires to maintain the integrity of the movements, attention should also be paid to following each other up and down, consistent with the hands and feet, and reaching the combination of hands and feet, elbows and knees. Shoulder and crotch requirements.

(8) *Coordinated respiration*

Practice should focus on breathing coordination. Inhale when actions stretching or rising, and exhale when actions going down or bending inwards in practicing Fitness Qigong. The coordination of breath should be based on the principle of nature and the premise of skillful movements.

4. Physiological effects of body adjustment

Body adjustment plays different physiological roles in dynamic exercise and motionless exercise. The body adjustment with the dynamic exercise refers to the regular movements of the whole body under the guidance of consciousness. The regular exercise refers to self-training according to a certain rhythm by composing the exercise routine which has a specific fitness function. The guiding motion of the routine is not a simple reflex movement, nor is it a formalized motion, but a complex intentional movement since the movements that make up the routine are rarely used in ordinary labor or sports activities. Each guiding motion is carried out in a broad network of activities regulated by nerves and muscles. The first step is that the cerebral cortex, the subcortical basal ganglia, and the cerebellum make motion planning, then the motor area of the cerebral cortex issues the motor command, and the brainstem and spinal cord motor neurons are responsible for the exercise. In order to correct the movement deviation in real-time and ensure the precision of adjustment, the complex feedback activities composed of all levels of motor center and peripheral receptors should be initiated.

静功调身的目的是将身体各个部位保持在最适生理状态，以放松肢体和调整呼吸，从而使大脑迅速进入并保持入静状态。人体生活在地球重力场之中，要维持正常的生理活动，大脑皮层就必须根据本体感受器的上行神经信息，协调全身神经和肌肉系统的活动，时时变换身体的姿势。若不对身姿进行约束和调整，就会使大脑皮层频受上行神经冲动的干扰，难以达到气功锻炼要求的放松和入静。因此，静功通过保持特定肢体姿势不变进行调身，实际上能使本体感受器上行到大脑皮层的神经冲动减少，从而有助于练功入静。

The purpose of motionless adjustment is to keep all parts of the body in an optimal physiological state to relax the limbs and adjust the breathing so that the brain quickly enters and maintains a static state. The human body lives in the gravity field of the earth. In order to maintain normal physiological activity, the cerebral cortex must coordinate the activities of the whole body nerve and muscle system according to the information offered by the ascending nerve of the proprioceptor, and change the posture of the body from time to time. If the posture is not constrained and adjusted, the cerebral cortex will be frequently disturbed by the upward nerve impulse, so it is difficult to achieve the Qigong exercise requirements of relaxation and quietness. Therefore, static/motionless exercises by keeping the posture of a particular limb unchanged, in fact, can reduce the nerve impulses of the proprioceptor ascending to the cerebral cortex, thus helping to practice into quietness.

第二要素：调息

调息是习练健身气功的重要环节和方法。古人说"一呼一吸谓之息"。所谓息，不仅是指呼和吸的过程，而且还指一呼一吸之间的停顿。调息就是指主动地、自觉地调整和控制呼吸的次数、深度等，并使之符合练功的要求和目的。

Element 2　Respiration Adjustment

The respiration adjustment is an important link and method for practicing Fitness Qigong. It is said in ancient time that "to inhale and exhale is called respiration." So respiration, not only refers to the process of exhaling and inhaling, but also includes the pause between exhaling and inhaling. Respiration adjustment refers to the active and conscious adjustment and control of breathing frequency, depth, and so on, in line with the requirements and objectives of the practice.

一、调息的作用

（1）用于止念

练功时如果安静不下来，可以把精神集中到呼吸上，借助调息来入静。方法是当意念随着呼吸运动时，一开始可

1. Roles of respiration adjustment

(1) *Used to stop thinking*

If one cannot calm down during the exercise, he can concentrate on breathing, to reach quiet with the help of respiration adjustment. The method is

以集中到呼吸所带来的形体运动上，注意吸气、呼气时胸部和腹部的起伏；再进一步，须把意念集中到呼吸出入的气流上，意念随呼吸的气流而上下移动，这样当精神全部集中到呼吸上时，意念自然也就系住了。

that when the mind moves with breathing, it can initially concentrate on the body movement driven by breathing, focusing on the ups and downs of the chest and abdomen when inhaling and exhaling; then concentrate on the airflow from the breathing, and the mind moves up and down with the airflow of breathing, so that when the whole mind concentrates on the breath, the consciousness is naturally tied.

(2) 吐故纳新

通过习练健身气功进行有意识地呼吸锻炼，可使人体更有效地吸入大自然的清气，呼出体内的浊气，达到吐故纳新，调节改善人体呼吸系统功能及各组织器官生理功能。

(2) *Exhale the old and inhale the new*

Conscious breathing exercise through practicing Fitness Qigong can help the human body to inhale the fresh air from nature more effectively, and exhale the foul air in the body, so as to regulate and improve the respiratory system function of the human body and the physiological functions of various tissues and organs.

(3) 行气活血

中医学认为，气为血之帅，血为气之母。呼吸是体内真气运行的主要动力，而真气又是血液运行的动力。因此，呼吸的练习，可以促进体内真气的发生、发展及全身血液的运行和输布，起到行气活血的作用。

(3) *Promoting Qi to activate blood*

TCM (Traditional Chinese Medicine) believes that Qi is the commander of blood, and blood is the source of Qi. Breathing is the main driving force for the movement of the genuine Qi in the body, and the genuine Qi is the power for the movement of the blood. Therefore, breathing practice can promote the occurrence, development of the genuine Qi, and the running, transportation and distribution of the whole body blood, and plays the role of promoting Qi and blood circulation.

(4) 强壮脏腑

古人说"呼出心与肺，吸入肝与肾"，呼吸长短、深浅、粗细的不同，可以直接影响相应脏腑的功能。现代医学认为，经常进行深长的呼吸锻炼，使横膈肌的升降幅度增大，改变了腹腔的内压，腹腔内压周期性的变动能"按摩"肠胃，促进肠胃蠕动，从而改善肠胃及内脏器官的功能。

(4) *Strengthening viscera*

It is said that "exhaling influences the heart and lung, inhaling influences the liver and kidney". Different breath length, depth, thickness can directly affect the functions of the corresponding viscera. Modern medicine believes that frequent deep and long breathing exercises can increase the amplitude of movement of the diaphragmatic muscle and change the intraperitoneal pressure. The periodic change of the intraperitoneal pressure can "massage" the intestines and stomach and promote the peristalsis of the intestines and stomach, thus to improve the function of intestines, stomach and internal organs.

二、调息的方法

调息的具体方法很多，根据习练健身气功功法的不同需要，可以选练不同的方法。常用的方法有：

（1）自然呼吸

在练功中采用日常生活的频率进行呼吸为自然呼吸法，不加意念支配，实质上是不调息而息自调。对于健身气功初学者来说，过分注意对呼吸的各种要求，执意调整，反而会顾此失彼，成为精神上的负担，出现不应有的紧张，以致呼吸反不顺畅。

（2）腹式呼吸

练功中通过横膈肌的运动来完成的呼吸为腹式呼吸法。腹式呼吸又分为顺腹式呼吸和逆腹式呼吸。

① 顺腹式呼吸：生理学上也称为等容呼吸，吸气时，腹肌放松，横膈肌随之下降，腹壁逐渐鼓起；呼气时，腹肌收缩，腹壁回缩或稍内凹，横膈肌也随之上升还原。这种呼吸不仅可以加大肺的换气量，而且对腹腔内脏起到按摩作用。

② 逆腹式呼吸：生理学上也称为变容呼吸。吸气时，腹肌收缩，腹壁回缩或稍内凹，横膈肌随之收缩下降，使腹腔容积变小；呼气时，腹肌放松，腹壁隆起，横膈肌上升还原，使腹腔容积变大。逆腹式呼吸对于内脏器官的影响较大，有类似按摩或运动内脏的作用，尤其对于改善肠胃功能有较大的帮助。

2. Methods of respiration adjustment

There are many specific methods for respiration adjustment. According to the different needs of practicing Qigong, different methods can be chosen. Common methods are as following:

(1) *Natural breathing*

In practice, to breathe according to the frequency of daily life without thoughts is the natural breathing method, which in essence is not the respiration adjustment but self-adjustment. If Fitness Qigong beginners pay too much attention to the various requirements of breathing, and insist on adjustment, on the contrary, they will lose one or another, and get a spiritual burden for themselves, which will cause undue tension to make respiration not smooth.

(2) *Abdominal respiration*

In practice, the abdominal breathing is performed through the movement of the diaphragm. It can be divided into cis-abdominal respiration and reverse abdominal respiration.

① The cis-abdominal respiration is also known as isovolumetric respiration physiologically. When inhaling, the abdominal muscle relaxes, the diaphragm decreases, and the abdominal wall gradually bulges; when exhaling, the abdominal muscle shrinks, the abdominal wall retracts or slightly concaves, and the diaphragmatic muscle rises and restores. This breathing not only increases lung volume, but also massages the celiac viscera.

② The reverse abdominal respiration is also known as volume change breathing physiologically. When inhaling, the abdominal muscle shrinks, and the abdominal wall retracts or slightly concaves, the diaphragm muscle shrinks too, and abdominal capacity becomes smaller; when exhaling, the abdominal muscle relaxes, the abdominal wall bulges, and the diaphragm rises and restores, making abdominal capacity larger. Reverse abdominal respiration has a great effect on internal organs, like massage or movement of viscera, especially for improving the function of intestines and stomach.

(3) 提肛呼吸

练功中把提肛动作和呼吸配合起来的练习方法称为提肛呼吸法。提肛呼吸是在吸气时有意识地收提肛门及会阴部肌肉，呼气时则放松肛门及会阴部肌肉。如"健身气功·五禽戏"中的猿提动作即是运用的这种呼吸方法。

(3) *Respiration with the levator ani sports*

In practice, the combination of the levator ani sports and breathing is called the respiration with the levator ani sports. It is the conscious shrink of anal and perineal muscles while inhaling and relaxation of anal and perineal muscles during exhalation. For example, ape-shrink motion adopts this breathing method in the "Fitness Qigong · Five Animal Exercises".

(4) 鼻吸口呼

健身气功的呼吸，一般要求鼻吸鼻呼法。但练功中呼气吐音，运气发声时可采用鼻吸口呼的方法。

(4) *Nasal respiration*

Fitness Qigong respiration generally requires nasal respiration method. However, in practice exhalation and phonation can be fulfilled through inhaling with noses and exhaling with mouths.

三、调息的要求

呼吸锻炼掌握得好，有利于整个练功的进行。如运用不当，也容易出现一些副作用，影响练功的正常进行及效果的获得。呼吸的锻炼，要注意把握以下一些基本的要求。

3. Requirements for respiration adjustment

The well-mastered breathing exercise is conducive to the entire exercise of the performance. If used improperly, it is easy to appear some side-effects, which affects the effect of exercise. So during breathing exercises, the following basic requirements are needed.

(1) 在松静的基础上调息

健身气功的调息，无论选择哪一种呼吸方法，都必须在松静的基础上进行练习。如果形体尤其是腰部不放松，气就不容易下沉，此时若强行运用腹式呼吸练功，则练功者容易出现憋气、胸闷等现象；若练功者情绪不安宁即进行调息锻炼，呼吸就不容易做到深、细、匀、长的要求。因此，要做到平心静气、心平气和。

(1) *To adjust the respiration in a relaxing surrounding*

The respiration adjustment in Fitness Qigong, no matter which breathing method is adopted, must practice in a relaxing surrounding. If the body, especially the waist cannot be relaxed, Qi is not easy to sink. in this case if the abdominal breathing exercise is forced to use, it is easy to cause suffocation, chest distress; if the mood is restless during the exercise, breathing cannot meet the requirements of being deep, thin, even, and long easily. Therefore, it is necessary to keep calm and patient.

(2) 不要盲目追求

所谓不能盲目追求，有两方面含义：一是指调息的方法，不能随意地选择与自身水平不相符合的调息方法；二是指调息的境界与效果，不能要求即刻见效，有了贪的思想，进行不切实际的

(2) *No blind pursuing*

"No blind pursuing" has two implications: first, it refers to that the methods of respiration adjustment cannot be chosen arbitrarily, which does not accord with the learner's own level; second, refers to that the realm and effect of the respiration adjustment,

追求，反而没有锻炼效果。

（3）不要强求深、细、匀、长

调息的深、细、匀、长是长期练出来的，这要有一个过程，不可能一蹴而就。如何才能达到深、细、匀、长，需要从自然呼吸调起。在进行自然呼吸时，慢慢把意念与呼吸结合在一起，随呼吸而出入，即做到心安气自调。因此，调息和入静是相辅相成的，心静以后呼吸也会逐渐变得深、细、匀、长。如果两者结合得不好，就会使得息不调、神不静，甚至会出现憋气等现象。

（4）精神与气息相合

练功中调息不是单纯做呼吸运动，而是着眼于呼吸的气息出入及意念集中呼吸运动的节律上，即把自己的意念活动和呼吸运动或气息的出入紧密结合起来，这样不但可以收摄心神，而且可以激发真气的产生。

（5）注意呼吸道的调整

呼吸道的调整主要对喉部而言。喉头回缩，下颌贴胸，两腮微微下落，使得喉咙通气道变小，呼吸气流变细。

（6）注意发音的口型

一般说不发音的调息要注意呼或吸的气息调整，而发音的呼或吸的动作要严格注意发音的口型。

总之，活泼自然是调息的基本要求。活泼就是不要把意识死死扣在呼吸

cannot be reached immediately. If the result is pursued greedily and impractically, it will be in vain.

（3） *No imposition for the respiration to be deep, thin, even, and long*

The deep, thin, even and long respiration is the result of long-term training, which can be reached with a long process, instead of overnight. How to achieve the result of deep, thin, even and long respiration should be begun with the natural breathing. In the process of the natural breathing, the mind and breathing are slowly combined, and inhaling and exhaling can help achieve the respiration adjustment with peaceful mind. Therefore, the respiration adjustment and calm mind are complementary. The calm mind can help the breathing gradually become deep, thin, even and long. If the two do not combine well, the dissonance, restlessness, and even suffocating will be caused.

（4） *Combination of spirit and respiration*

In practice, the respiration adjustment is not simply a breathing exercise, but rather focuses on the action of inhaling and exhaling, and the rhythm of the mind-concentrating respiration, that is, the respiratory movement or breath should closely be combined with the mental activity. This can not only help to concentrate, but also stimulate the production of the genuine air in the body.

（5） *Adjustment of respiratory tract*

Respiratory adjustment mainly refers to the larynx adjustment. The throat retracts, the lower jaw adheres to the chest, and the cheeks fall slightly, thus making the throat airway narrower and breathing airstream thinner.

（6） *The mouth shape with pronunciation*

Generally speaking, it is necessary to adjust inhaling or exhaling during the aphonic respiration, and necessary to pay attention to the mouth shape strictly during the pronunciation respiration.

In short, being vivacious and natural is the basic requirements for the respiration adjustment. Vivacity doesn't

运动上，而是顺其自然、循序渐进地调理呼吸运动和气息，自然地逐步达到形、气、神三者合一的状态，切忌刻意追求，生搬硬套。

四、调息的生理作用

正常情况下的呼吸是一种受控于延髓和桥脑的自动节律性活动，但由于呼吸肌是骨骼肌，也能够直接受大脑皮层的控制做随意性呼吸。因此，调息可分为自动调息和主动调息两种形式。

（1）自动调息

自主呼吸运动的基本意义是保障肺内与外界的气体交换，从而有效地提供机体代谢所需的氧气并排出体内产生的二氧化碳。练功过程中呼吸运动自动配合练功的节奏，静功呼吸缓慢深沉，动功呼吸频率加快、通气量增大，以便保障练功过程的能量代谢需求。这种自动形式的调息过程，是通过神经体液的调节机制实现的。练功过程的代谢活动改变了血液中氧和二氧化碳分压比例，这种变化通过颈动脉和延髓的化学感受器上传，经过呼吸中枢的整合发出调整节律的指令。正常情况下，自主呼吸运动仅受延髓和桥脑呼吸中枢的调控，不向大脑皮层发放激惹性神经冲动。自动调息的这一特点可用来协助练功入静：将静功锻炼的意念集中于呼吸的自动节律上，通过数息或墨守等方法，不仅能够使大脑皮层减少因呼吸方式变更而产生的上行神经冲动的干扰，而且已有的意念活动也将随呼吸的自动节律而逐渐单一，直至止念入静。

mean that the mind has to follow the breathing movements strictly, but to conform to nature, gradually adjusting the breathing movements and respiration to achieve the state of form, Qi, God in one. Do not deliberately pursue, and apply mechanically.

4. Physiological function of respiration adjustment

Normal breathing is an automatic rhythmic activity controlled by the medulla oblongata and pons, but because the respiratory muscle is a skeletal muscle, it can also be directly controlled by the cerebral cortex to make the random breathing. Therefore, the respiration adjustment can be divided into two forms: automatic respiration adjustment and active respiration adjustment.

(1) *Automatic respiration adjustment*

The basic significance of autonomic respiratory movement is to ensure the air exchange between the lungs and the outside world so as to effectively provide the oxygen required for metabolism and discharge the carbon dioxide produced in the body. In order to guarantee the energy metabolism demand for the exercise process, the breathing movement automatically cooperates with the rhythm of the exercise, the breathing rate of the static work/exercise is slow and deep, the breathing frequency of the exercise work is speeded up, and the ventilation volume is increased. This form of the automatic respiration adjustment process is achieved through the regulation mechanism of neurohumoral fluid. The metabolic activities during exercise change the ratio of the partial pressure of oxygen to carbon dioxide in the blood, which is uploaded through chemosensors in the carotid artery and medulla oblongata and sent out through the integration of the respiratory center command to adjust the rhythm. Normally, the autonomic respiratory movement is regulated only by the medulla oblongata and pons respiratory center, and does not release irritating nerve impulses to the cerebral cortex. This feature of automatic respiration adjustment can be used to help the practice get into calmness: to concentrate the idea of static exercise on the automatic rhythm of breathing by means of counting or keeping calm. Not only can the cerebral cortex reduce the disturbance of the ascending nerve impulses caused by the change of breathing mode, but also the existing mental activity will become single gradually with the automatic rhythm of respiration until the thought is stopped.

(2) 主动调息

不同呼吸频率和呼吸深度,吸与呼的不同比例,以及呼吸周期与意念和发音的不同组合等,可以构成多种多样的主动调息形式。历代有关调息方法的记述多达50余种,足见主动调息在气功锻炼中的重要地位。主动调息具有定向影响自主神经调节功能的作用。实验显示、长吸短呼的方法不仅造成吸气中枢的兴奋优势,而且这种优势能扩散到整个交感神经系统,造成交感神经系统的兴奋优势;反之,长呼短吸的调息方法将造成呼气中枢的兴奋优势,并进而出现副交感神经系统的兴奋优势。可见,随着呼吸频率及呼吸活动形式的不同,机体的植物性神经功能状态亦不相同。鉴于自主神经系统在机体自我调节功能中的核心地位,调息则可凭借对自主神经功能的作用,将其影响扩大到人体的各个器官和系统。现代医学认为,个人意识无法直接影响内脏器官的活动,患病时只能采用药化或物理手段进行治疗。但实际上,聪明的古人早已巧妙地利用了呼吸的随意性特点,通过对呼吸方式的直接干预,间接地对内脏功能产生影响,达到祛病健身的效果。

(2) Active respiration adjustment

Different respiratory rates and depth, different proportions of inhalation and exhalation, and different combinations of respiratory cycle and ideation and pronunciation can form a variety of active breath adjustment forms. There are more than 50 kinds of methods of respiration adjustment in the past dynasties, which shows that active respiration adjustment plays an important role in the Qigong exercise. The active respiration adjustment has the function of directionally affecting the orienteering function for the vegetative nerves. The experiment shows that the method of long inhalation and short exhalation not only causes the excitation advantage of inspiratory center, but also spread to the whole sympathetic nervous system, resulting in the excitation advantage of the sympathetic nervous system. On the contrary, the respiration adjustment method of long exhalation and short inhalation will give the expiratory center the excitement advantage, and then the excitement advantage of the parasympathetic nervous system appears. It can be seen that the state of vegetative nerve function varies with the changes in the respiratory frequency and activity. In view of the central position of the vegetative nervous system in the self-regulating function of the body, the respiration adjustment can extend its influence to the various organs and systems of the human body by virtue of its effect on the function of the vegetative nervous system. Modern medicine holds that individual consciousness cannot directly affect the activities of internal organs and can only be treated with the pharmacy or physical treatment means. But in fact, the wise ancients have skillfully taken advantage of the random nature of breathing. Through direct intervention in the way of breathing, the visceral function is indirectly influenced to achieve the effect of fitness and eliminating diseases.

第三要素：调心

调心是调身和调息的核心。所谓调心是指练功者在健身气功锻炼中，对自我的精神意识、思维活动进行调整和运用，以达到练功的要求和目的。

一、调心的作用

调心基本内容可概括为"意守"二字，即意念归一，是非强制性的注意力集中。这种意念活动的特征在于轻松的专一，排除杂念，以防散乱。从此可以引申出广义的调心，主要是正确地认识客观规律，从而保持健康的心理状态，能对自己实行合理的心理控制和行为控制。现代研究认为，心理活动对生理活动有不可忽视的影响，只有健康的心理状态才能保证身体健康。实验和事实证明，人的意念活动也能间接支配自主神经系统管理的内脏活动，通过意守、入静这种"反身注意"和心理暗示，可调节许多生理功能。从心理学角度分析，意守可以锻炼注意力和想象力两种重要的心理品质。

二、调心的方法

调心的方法主要是"意守"。意守的方法虽然很多，但不外乎三个方面：从意守对象说，可以守虚也可守实，可以守有也可守无；以人体内外分，有守外景与内景之别；景象又可分为动象与静象。根据目前的教学实践和经验，意守的具体方法有以下几个方面。

Element 3   Mind Adjustment

The mind adjustment is the core of body adjustment and respiration adjustment. Mind adjustment refers to the adjustment and application of self-consciousness and thinking activities in the exercise of Qigong in order to achieve the requirements and purposes of practice.

1. Effect of mind adjustment

The basic content of the mind adjustment can be summarized as the word "mind concentration", that is to say, the idea is unified as one and non-mandatory concentration of attention. This activity is characterized by easy concentration, eliminating confusion and preventing confusion. So it can be extended to the broad sense of the mind adjustment, mainly understanding the objective law correctly to maintain a healthy psychological state, and be able to make self-control for reasonable psychological activities and behavior. Modern research suggests that psychological activities have a nonnegligible influence on physiological activities, and only a healthy psychological state can guarantee physical health. Experiments and facts have proved that human mental activities can also indirectly dominate the visceral activities controlled by the vegetative nervous system, and can regulate many physiological functions through the "reflexive attention" and a psychological hint of mind-keeping, which is known as "mind concentration" and "keeping calm". From a psychological point of view, the mind concentration can promote two important psychological qualities of attention and imagination.

2. Ways of mind adjustment

The main way to adjust the mind is to stick to it (mind concentration). Although there are many ways of mind concentration, there are mainly three aspects: from the point of view of the object of the mind concentration, it is possible to keep virtual or true, or to keep the exist or nothing; to divide, there is the difference between keeping the exterior and the interior based on the inside and outside of the body; and the exterior and the interior scene can be the moving images or the still images. According to the current teaching practice and experience, the specific methods of mind concentration have the following aspects.

(1) 意守身体放松法

在保证身形和动作姿态正确的前提下，有意识地放松身体是练功中最基本的方法。从练功一开始，就要精神放松，思想集中，呼吸调匀，同时诱导身体各部位从上到下，从里到外，四肢百骸，五脏六腑进行放松，使其舒适自然，毫无紧张之感准备练功。在动作练习过程中，不断保持并尽可能使这种放松的程度加深，既解除各种紧张状态，也要做到松而不懈。这种有意识地放松精神和肢体，就是意念集中的一种表现。

(1) Mind concentration on body relaxation

On the premise that body shape and posture are correct, consciously relaxing the body is the most basic method in the practice of Qigong. From the beginning of the exercise, it is necessary to relax, concentrate, and breathe evenly, and at the same time induce all parts of the body to relax from the top to the bottom, from the inside to the outside, from the extremities to the outside, to relax the five viscera, to make it comfortable and natural, and to prepare for the exercise without a sense of tension. In the process of exercise, keep and make the degree of relaxation deepen as far as possible, not only relieve all kinds of tension, but also keeping relaxing without being sluggish. This conscious relaxation of the mind and body is a manifestation of concentration.

(2) 意守身体部位法

意守可以意守自己身体的某一部位，但常用的意守部位一般是经络上的穴位。通过意守身体上的某一穴位，不仅有助于排除杂念，而且由于意守穴位的不同，也有助于疏通气血和调节脏腑的功能。通常意守的穴位有丹田、百会、命门、会阴、涌泉、劳宫、少商等，其他穴位也可根据情况灵活选用。

(2) Mind concentration on body parts

Mind concentration can be conducted on a certain part of the body, commonly on the acupoint of the part. It not only helps to eliminate miscellaneous thoughts, but also helps to promote the flow of Qi and blood and regulate the function of viscera through different acupoints. Usually, the acupoints for the mind concentration are Dantian, Baihui, Mengmen, perineum, Yongquan, Laogong, Shaoshang, etc. Of course, other acupoints can also be used flexibly according to the situation.

(3) 意守体外对象法

大自然的万事万物都可以作为体外的意守对象，大则日月星辰、山川湖海，小到花草树木等。但选择的意守对象内容要简单，自己要熟悉，对自己有吸引力，能使自己心情愉快，那些刺激性强、扰动性大、会引起高度兴奋的事物，不宜作为意守对象。

(3) Mind concentration in vitro

Everything in nature can be used as an external object of the mind concentration, including the sun and moon, mountains, lakes and oceans, flowers, grass, trees, and so on. But the choice of the intended object should be simple, familiar, and attractive to learners themselves, which can make them in a good mood. The strongly irritating, disturbing or exciting objects, cannot be used in the mind concentration.

另外，在练功实践中还有三种常用的意守方法。

① 意想动作过程。在练功过程中意想动作规格是否正确，方法是否准确清晰，练功要领是否得法，既可集中意念，也可达到正确地掌握功法技术。

② 意想呼吸。这是练功中有意识地注意呼吸的一种练习方法，常用的有数息法、随息法、听息法等。

③ 注意默念字句。默念的字句要简单，做到声发于口，闻之于耳，察之于心。默念字句除能集中精神外，还可通过声符振动和暗示作用，收到安定精神、调整气血的效果。

三、调心的要求

调心的基本要求是"入静"，即思想上进入一种安静的状态。医家经典《素问·上古天真论》曰："恬淡虚无，真气从之。"恬是安静，淡是朴素，虚无则不为物欲所蔽。恬淡以养神，虚无以养志，这就达到了调心的目的。

一般来说，入静在练功者的功法掌握，练功质量都比较好的情况下才能出现。因此，入静是通过练功实践得来的，通过功夫积累得来的，是在有意识的锻炼中、无意识的情况下形成而出现的。由于每个练功者的练功情况不同，每一种功法的情况也不全部相似，入静的程度和境界也就有所差异。初学健身

In addition, there are three common methods in the practice of mind concentration.

① Motions in the mind concentration. In the process of practicing the mind concentration, it is necessary to think about whether the specification of action is correct or not, whether the method is accurate and clear, and whether the practicing essentials are right or not, which can not only help concentrate on the idea, but also master the technique of the practice method correctly.

② Respiration in the mind concentration. This is the practice of conscious attention to breathing in practice. Commonly learners are requested to count, follow and listen to the breathing.

③ Concentration on the meditation of words. Words for meditation should be simple, pronounced from the mouth, heard with the ears, understood in the mind. Meditation of words cannot only help focus on the spirit, but also through note vibration and hint, the effect of the spirit of tranquility and the Qi and blood adjustment can be reached.

3. Requirements for mind concentration

The basic requirement for the mind concentration is to enter into calmness, that is to say, to enter a quiet state of mind. The medical classic book "*Plain Questions*" says that "The genuine air follows tranquility and nihility." Tranquility means to be quiet in the mind and simple; nihility means not being blinded by material desire. Tranquility helps to repose, and nihility to strengthen the will. This is the purpose of the mind concentration.

Generally speaking, entering and keeping calmness will appear only under the situation of the practitioner's master of the skills, and the relatively good quality of practice. Therefore, entering and keeping calmness is gained and accumulated through practice, formed in conscious exercise and appears unconsciously. Because each practitioner's practice situation is different and the situation of each kind of practice

气功，不可对入静要求过高，以致产生急躁情绪，反而难以入静。只要姿势自然舒适，呼吸柔和，思想上的各种杂念相对减少，或者起了念头能很快地排除就算入静了。随着练功的深入，便逐渐过渡到对外界的声音干扰，闻如不闻，身体轻松，呼吸绵绵，意念归一的状态。甚至做到呼吸绵绵深长，用意自如，练功结束好似沐浴过后，心情舒畅，精神饱满。当然，这些入静状态并非每一次功法锻炼都能出现，有时偶尔出现，有时常常来临，有时交替反复。它也不可能完全如上述描述那样线条明晰，需要练功者多加细心体会。

当然，这些入静状态并非每一次功法锻炼都能出现，有时偶尔出现，有时常常来临，有时交替反复。它也不可能完全如上述描述那样线条明晰，需要练功者多加细心体会。

避免追求是入静中要注意的主要问题。因为追求本身就是一种意念活动，是一种兴奋状态，它必然影响入静的出现与持续。在入静过程中，如果被感觉所吸引，被舒服所吸引，企求入静状态能持续下去，这样反会中断原来的入静。因为原来的入静状态，被新建立的企求兴奋灶所排挤、破坏而弄巧成拙。练功者应该自然地保存原来的入静状态，在不企求的情况下，自然能够达到预想的目的。

健身气功功法繁多，但调身、调息、调心的基本要素是共同的。三调之间是相互依存和相互制约的关系，调身是基础，调息是中介，调心主导调身和调息。每一种健身气功功法，每一次健身气功锻炼的过程，都是这三者的具体结合与运用。

method is not all similar, the degree and the realm of entering and keeping calmness also vary a lot. Beginners of Fitness Qigong cannot have too high requirements for entering and keeping calmness to generate an impatient mood, which is difficult for entering and keeping calmness. As long as the posture is natural and comfortable, the breathing is soft, the distracting thoughts are relatively reduced, or the sudden thoughts can quickly be excluded, entering and keeping calmness is fulfilled. With the deepening of practice, gradually the outside sound interference is smell not heard, the body is relaxed, and breathing gentle and long without pauses, the mind free and energetic.

Of course, not in every exercise entering and keeping calmness can occur. Sometimes it happens occasionally, sometimes often, and sometimes alternately. Its occurrence cannot be as clear as the above description. It requires more careful experience by the practitioners.

Avoiding pursuing is the main problem that should be paid attention to in entering and keeping calmness. The pursuit itself is a kind of mental activity, is a kind of excitement, which inevitably influences the appearance and the continuation of entering and keeping calmness. In the process of entering and keeping calmness, if the practitioners are attracted by the feeling, by the comfort, by the desire to maintain the static state, the original entry will be interrupted because the original static state will be crowded out and damaged by the newly established excitatory desire. The practitioner should naturally preserve the original static state without any desire to achieve the desired purpose.

There are many methods of Fitness Qigong, but the basic elements for the body adjustment, respiration adjustment and mind adjustment are the same. The relationship among the three tunes is interdependent and restricted mutually: the body adjustment is the basis, respiration adjustment is the intermediary, and the mind adjusting dominates the body adjustment and respiration adjustment. Each kind of fitness Qigong method, every Fitness Qigong exercise process, is the concrete combination and application of these three.

四、调心的生理作用

健身气功通过神经体液调节引发生理和心理效应之间有着良性的相互关系，即良好的生理效应有助于良好的心理效应的出现，而良好心理效应的保持也会促进更好的生理效应。大脑有两个部位与气功锻炼密切相关，一个是前脑额叶，另一个是脑垂体。前脑额叶是人类高级神经活动的场所，不仅控制着人的意识活动，而且参与内脏的功能调节。临床脑电图学的观察资料表明，人在环境安舒、心情愉悦时，α频段脑波增多；而在焦虑紧张时，则β频段脑波增多。说明从颅骨表面记录到的脑电波变化能够反映大脑皮层的功能活动。脑垂体是人体神经体液调节系统的控制中枢，在调控人体生理、心理机能方面具有重要作用。两种由脑垂体管控的神经介质可以把人的身心关系联系在一起，一种是能够产生愉悦感的类吗啡物质，另一种化学物质是去甲肾上腺素。有关实验表明，这两种脑内激素的分泌与情绪有关。当人的情绪愉快、α频段脑波增加时，能够促进β-内啡肽分泌；而当人的心情焦虑、β频段脑波增加时，则会促进去甲肾上腺素的分泌。

有关气功锻炼过程脑电频谱分析的研究结果显示：受试者入静时，前脑额叶α频段脑波能量增大，并进一步出现全脑α节律同步化的现象；受试者对这

4. Physiological effect of mind adjustment

Fitness Qigong helps to establish a good relationship between physiological and psychological effects through the regulation of neurohumoral fluid, that is, good physiological effects contribute to the emergence of good psychological effects, and the maintenance of good psychological effects will also promote better physiological effects. There are two parts in the brain closely related to Qigong exercise, one is the frontal lobe, and the other is the pituitary gland. The prefrontal lobe is the site of human high-level neural activity, which not only controls human conscious activity, but also participates in the adjustment and regulation of visceral function. The observation data of clinical electroencephalography shows that when the environment is comfortable and the mood is happy, the α-band brain wave increases, while in the anxious and tense mood, the β-band brain waves increases. This indicates that the changes of brain waves recorded from the surface of the skull can reflect the functional activities of the cerebral cortex. The pituitary is the control center of the human neurohumoral regulation system, which plays an important role in regulating physiological and psychological functions of the human body. Two neurotransmitters controlled by the pituitary gland can link people's physical and mental relationships, one is a morphine-like substance that produces pleasure, and the other is norepinephrine. Experiments have shown that the secretion of these two brain hormones is related to emotion. When a person is happy and α-band brain wave increases, it can promote the secretion of β-endorphin, and when a person is anxious and the β-band brain wave increases, it stimulates the secretion of norepinephrine.

The results of EEG spectrum analysis on Qigong exercises show that the α-band energy in the frontal lobe has increased and the whole brain α-rhythm is synchronized when the subjects entered static state. The subjects' memories of the period were sweet with

一时段的回忆则是喜悦甘甜之感。根据练功者入静时的脑波变化和情绪状态分析，调心入静时前脑额叶的神经活动，促使脑垂体增加愉悦感的β-内啡肽分泌，进而通过遍布全身的受体，改善人体的自我调节功能，增强人体的自愈能力。此外，涵养道德是调心的重要内容，高尚的平稳心态可避免和应对外部环境的应激源，从而防止去甲肾上腺素过多分泌，保持人体的健康稳态。

joy. According to the change of brain wave and emotional state of the practitioner at the time of entering the quietness, the neural activity in the frontal lobe of the prefrontal lobe during the adjustment promotes the secretion of β-endorphin, and then improves the self-regulation function and self-healing ability of the human body through the self-receptors all over the body. In addition, the cultivation of morality is an important part of the mind adjustment. The noble and stable mentality can avoid and deal with the stress source from the external environment to prevent the excessive secretion of norepinephrine and maintain the healthy and steady-state of the human body.

第二章 健身气功·五禽戏概述
Chapter 2 Summary of Fitness Qigong · Wu Qin Xi

本章要点："健身气功·五禽戏"是众多健身气功项目中最具代表性的一套功法，简单易学，普及率高，在全民健身活动与对外文化交流中均发挥着不可替代的作用。本章主要从"健身气功·五禽戏"的功法源流、功法特点、习练要领这三个方面进行了详细论述。

Key points： "Fitness Qigong · Wu Qin Xi" is one of the most representative exercise methods among numerous Fitness Qigong events, which is easy and popular to learn, and plays an irreplaceable role in the national fitness activities and international cultural exchange. This chapter illustrates its three aspects in detail：its origin and development, features, and main exercise methods.

健身气功·五禽戏概述

第一节 功法起源

"五禽戏"又称"五禽操""五禽气功""百步汗戏"等。五禽戏的起源最早可追溯到中国的远古时代。

五禽戏是中国传统的运动养生功法，其发源地在许昌。据《后汉书·华佗传》记载，五禽戏由东汉时期的名医华佗创编。华佗根据"流水不腐，户枢不蠹"的思想创编的这套保健养生功法，是通过模仿五种动物的姿势、神态、秉性特征等，结合自身锻炼，活动筋骨血脉，促进消化、吸收，以达到增强体质、预防和治疗疾病的目的。

Section 1 Origin and Development of Exercise Methods

"Wu Qin Xi" (Five-animal Play), also known as "Wu Qin Cao" (Five animal Exercise), "Wu Qin Qigong", and "Baibu Han Xi" (Hundred-step Sweating Practice), can be traced back to the ancient times.

As one of the self-practice exercises for health maintenance and longevity, Wu Qin Xi was originated in a place called Xuchang. According to the statements of *Book of Later Han · Biography of Hua Tuo*, Wu Qin Xi was created by a famous physician of the Eastern Han Dynasty, Hua Tuo, who devised a set of exercises based on the idea of "Running water is never stale and a door-hinge never get worm eaten" in order to keep healthy and pursue longevity. By mimicking the posture, manner, and nature of the five animals, the whole set of exercises help to strengthen muscles, unfold tendons and joints, circulate qi and blood, and enhance digestion and absorption to meet the purpose of building up the body, and preventing and curing diseases.

"Fitness Qigong • Wu Qin Xi" was devised in the order of tiger, deer, bear, monkey, and bird as recorded in *Records of the Three Kingdoms • Biography of Hua Tuo*. The numbers of movements follow that recorded in *Records of Nourishing the Body and Extending Life* by Tao Hongjing of the Southern and Northern Dynasties, ten motions with two motions in each exercise. In addition, a starting posture for regulating breath and a closing posture for returning Qi to Dantian are added before and after a complete set of exercises, which makes twelve motions in total.

Section 2 Features of Exercise Methods

"Fitness Qigong • Wu Qin Xi" is a set of exercises with moderate intensity and simple movements, focusing on the balanced development of the body. There are twelve motions altogether and it takes about thirteen minutes to finish the whole set of exercises. Practitioners can choose one of the exercises for repeated practice, which all depends on individuals' physical bearing capacity or symptoms.

"Fitness Qigong • Wu Qin Xi" is a set of exercises, taking waist as the center, coordinating and mobilizing all meridians and doing overall exercises on Zang-fu organs, and improving the physiologic function of the body. By swaying and flexing body trunks, spines get regulated and exercised to stimulate Ren and Du Channels; by changing hand forms and varying stances, nerve endings of fingers and toes are activated to reinforce qi and blood circulation in the twelve meridians and improve the function of Zang-fu organs.

"Fitness Qigong • Wu Qin Xi" was called "Daoyin" in ancient China. It aims at improving health by external physical exercises and internal breath regulation to circulate blood and qi flow. Externally emphasis is given to mimic the features and characteristics of the

念的运用，习练时始终保持呼吸的通畅与意念的集中；动作熟练后，做到呼吸意念与动作达到协调一致、和谐统一。

"健身气功·五禽戏"的功法注重戏与戏之间的气息调整与心境的转换，通过两掌45°侧起、内收、下按，使身心得到短暂的静养与平和，起到过渡和调整的作用；在功法的开始和结束部分，增加专门的调息练习，能够使习练者快速进入练功状态或恢复常态。

第三节　习练要领

"健身气功·五禽戏"是一套以模仿动物为主的仿生类养生功法。练习者在习练过程中，要注意以下几个环节。

一、动作的外形

外形，也就是姿势、形态。五禽戏以模仿动物的形态为练习方式，每戏动作都有其特有的动作形态，练习时要准确把握动物的个性特征，体现动物的特点。如在虎戏中，有"虎爪"的上、下撑举与前扑、下按的动作，要体现出虎的力量和威猛；在猿戏中，通过撤步观望、上树摘果、捧果欣赏的环节，表现了猿生性多疑敏感而又动作敏捷、灵巧的特点。因此，在习练时，不仅要掌握外在动作，更要合乎其内在特质，达到形神兼备。

二、动作的神态与韵味

中国的古语有"相由心生"，意思是内在的思想、感情是能够转化为外在

five animals in nature. Internally attentions are given to regulating breathing and mind. During the practice, it is important to keep unobstructed breathing and mental focus. With more practice, harmonious integration of respiration, mind and movements will be achieved.

When practicing "Fitness Qigong · Wu Qin Xi", the emphasis is laid on regulating breathing and switching minds between exercises. The effects of transition and regulation can be achieved by raising both palms to the level of the chest with palms facing up at 45 degrees between body and arms, turning elbows inward and pushing palms down and resting them at the sides of the body to reach a quiet and peaceful body and mind for a short period. At the beginning and closing of each motion, a special exercise of regulating breath is added to lead practitioners to enter into a state of exercises or the normal state.

Section 3　Main Exercise Methods

"Fitness Qigong · Wu Qin Xi" is a set of bionic exercises on the life cultivation regimen. When practicing, the following needs focusing on.

1. Posture

Posture refers to the pose and stance. Since Wu Qin Xi is devised to mimic the movements of the five animals, when practicing practitioners are expected to imitate the movements of the five animals as closely as possible, trying to bear the temperaments and manner of the five animals. For example, tigers' power and the manner of mightiness and majesty are supposed to appear in Tiger Exercise. While in Monkey Exercise the manner of agility and quickness, and nature of glancing around are also expected to come out. Thus when practicing, both external movement features and internal temperaments and manner of the five animals are supposed to come into sight.

2. Spirit

There is an old saying in China, "The face is the index of the Mind", meaning inner thoughts and emo-

的表现，通过外在的行为能够窥见内心的想法和状态。五禽戏特别注重对动物神态的模仿，通过外在神态来体现其个性特征，疏泄内在情感，通调脏腑气机。所以说，神韵是练习五禽戏不可缺少的内容。

tions can be converted into outer looking or inner thoughts and state can be betrayed by outer appearance and behavior. In practicing Wu Qin Xi, much emphasis is laid on mimicking the spirit and manner of the animals. By imitating movements and manner of the animals, the features and personalities of animals could be reflected, inner emotions could be given vent to and functional activity of Zang-fu could be tuned. Thus spirit is indispensable to Wu Qin Xi.

三、对意念、意识，也就是思想的把握

在习练时，应集中精神，排除杂念，保持身心的高度统一与和谐。

3. Mind

Mind refers to the mental state of practitioners. In the exercise, practitioners are supposed to regulate mental activity and concentrate on one thought, get rid of all stray thoughts and integrate body, mind, and spirit into one.

四、呼吸的锻炼与调整

练功时针对呼吸的专门性练习，称为"调息"。调息练习，是气功练习中的重要内容，通过对呼吸的调整，将呼吸与意念、动作紧密结合，达到缓慢、匀细、深长的程度，以利身体健康。初学者应先学会动作，明确其含义，使姿势达到舒适、准确，待身体放松、情绪安定后，逐渐注意调整呼吸。

4. Respiration

When practicing Fitness Qigong, a specialized breathing training called "regulating the breath" is needed. Breathing is a crucial component in qigong practice. By conscious regulating the depth, frequency, and rhythm of respiration and gradual integrating breathing with mind and movements, practitioners are expected to achieve a finer, softer even deeper breathing. For beginners, the first step is to understand the connotation of the movements and then learn to do them correctly and comfortably, and only when the movements are performed with a relaxed body and ease mind then can be given care to adjusting the breath.

第三章　健身气功·五禽戏动作图解
Chapter 3　The Movement Illustration of Fitness Qigong·Wu Qin Xi

本章要点：本章通过 85 幅动作图片和 8 段高清视频（视频全部配有中英文字幕）详细讲述了健身气功五禽戏功法的基本功和全套动作的练习方法。

Key points：The chapter introduces detailedly the basic techniques for practicing the Five-Animal Exercises in Fitness Qigong with 85 motion diagrams and 8 HD videos accompanied with Chinese and English subtitles.

第一节　基本功

一、手型

（1）虎爪

　　五指撑开，屈指内收，稍加力，掌心松空（图 3-1）。

（2）鹿角

　　拇指、食指、小指伸直，中指、无名指屈指内扣，虎口打开（图 3-2）。

Section 1　Basic Techniques

1. Hands

（1）*Tiger's paw*

Spread fingers and thumb, forming a semicircle with index finger and thumb, the rest fingers bending inward with a hollow and relaxed center of the palm (Fig. 3-1).

（2）*Deer's antler*

Straighten thumb, index and little fingers with middle and ring fingers bending inward, stretching the distance between thumb and index fingers (Fig. 3-2).

图 3-1　(Fig. 3-1)

图 3-2　(Fig. 3-2)

（3）熊掌

四指并拢内屈,拇指指腹压在食指指甲部位,虎口微撑（图3-3）。

（4）猿钩

屈腕,五指自然微弯,指腹捏拢（图3-4）。

（3）*Bear's paw*

Form a circle with the tip of thumb pressing against that of the index finger, keeping four fingers close together while bending them (Fig. 3-3).

（4）*Monkey's hooked paw*

Keep the inner sides of tips of all fingers and thumb together with the wrist flexed (Fig. 3-4).

图3-3　(Fig. 3-3)

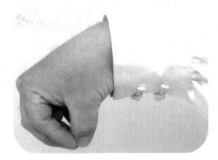

图3-4　(Fig. 3-4)

（5）鸟翅

五指伸直、分开,拇指、食指、小指上翘,无名指、中指并拢下压（图3-5）。

（6）握固

拇指按压无名指指根处,四指并拢内屈,收于掌心（图3-6）。

（5）*Bird's wing*

Extend fingers, with thumb, index and little fingers tilted and middle and ring fingers staying together and bending downward (Fig. 3-5).

（6）*Solid fist*

Press the tip of thumb against the proximal end of the ring finger, then bend all fingers and cover thumb (Fig. 3-6).

图3-5　(Fig. 3-5)

图3-6　(Fig. 3-6)

二、步型

（1）弓步

两腿前后分开约一腿长,横向距离

2. Stance

（1）*Bow stance*

Put one foot forward with tiptoes facing forward, keep-

约一脚长；前脚脚尖朝正前，前腿膝关节弯曲，呈屈蹲姿势，膝盖不过脚尖；后腿膝关节自然伸直，全脚掌着地，脚尖外开（图3-7）。

ing a leg distance lengthwise and a foot distance crosswise with the other, front knee bending with thigh slanting to the ground and knee above tiptoes; meanwhile, the other leg is stretching naturally with whole foot on the ground, tiptoes turning outward (Fig. 3-7).

图 3-7 （Fig. 3-7）

（2）虚步

前脚脚跟着地，勾脚尖，微屈膝；后腿屈膝下蹲，脚尖外开 45°，全脚掌着地；身体重心放于后腿（图3-8）。

（3）丁步

两脚左右分开，间距 1~2 横拳；两腿屈膝半蹲，左（右）脚脚跟提起，脚前掌虚点地面，位于右（左）脚脚心处，右（左）腿全脚掌着地踏实（图3-9）。

（2）*Empty stance*

Rest the heel of the front foot on the ground with tiptoes tilting upward and knee slightly bent; bend rear leg with whole foot on the ground and tiptoes turning outward 45 degrees. Bodyweight rests on the rear leg (Fig. 3-8).

（3）*T-stance*

Stand with feet 10-20cm apart, bend both legs half squatting, lift the heel of one foot with its tiptoes slightly touching the ground next to the arch of the other foot, which is solidly rested on the ground (Fig. 3-9).

图 3-8 （Fig. 3-8）

图 3-9 （Fig. 3-9）

三、平衡

（1）提膝平衡

左（右）腿直立站稳，上体正直；右（左）腿在体前屈膝上提，小腿自然下垂，脚尖向下（图3-10）。

（2）后举腿平衡

右（左）腿蹬直站稳，左（右）腿伸直，向体后举起，脚面绷直，脚尖向下（图3-11）。

3. Balance

（1） Balance with one knee lifted

Stand straight on one leg, and lift the knee of the other leg in front of the body, with shank naturally hanging down and tiptoes pointing to the ground (Fig. 3-10).

（2） Balance with one leg lifted backward

Stand still on one leg, and lift the other leg backward with foot stretching out and tiptoes pointing downward, keeping both legs straight (Fig. 3-11).

图3-10 （Fig. 3-10）

图3-11 （Fig. 3-11）

第二节　动作图解

预备势、起势调息

（1）动作

预备势　起势调息

动作一：两脚并拢，中正站立；两臂自然伸直，两手垂放于身体两侧，十指舒展，中指指尖轻贴裤缝处；头正颈直，下颌微内收，舌尖轻触上颚；松胸实腹，眼睛平视前方（图3-12）。

动作二：左脚向左侧开半步，约与肩同宽，自然站立；调匀呼吸，意守丹田

Section 2　Illustration of Movement

Ready Position Starting and Regulating Breath

（1） Actions

Action 1: Stand straight with two feet close to each other, drop two arms naturally to the sides of the body with ten fingers relaxed; erect head and neck, jaw drawn back a little and tongue touching the upper palate; chest in and qi in Dantian, and look straight ahead (Fig. 3-12).

Action 2: Set apart two feet by moving left foot half step left. The distance of feet is the same as shoul-

（图 3-13）。

ders. Regulate breathing to a uniform frequency with mind concentrating at Dantian (Fig. 3-13).

图 3-12　(Fig. 3-12)

图 3-13　(Fig. 3-13)

动作三：两臂外旋，上托至胸前膻中穴高度，掌心向上；眼睛跟随两手动作（图 3-14）。

动作四：两臂屈肘内合，转掌心向下，按至腹前；眼睛平视前方（图 3-15）。

Action 3: Raise both arms up to the front of the chest, the same level as Danzhong point with palms facing upward, eyes following hands (Fig. 3-14).

Action 4: Turn elbows inward, move palms closer to each other and turn them downward and lower them to the front of the abdomen; look straight ahead (Fig. 3-15).

图 3-14　(Fig. 3-14)

图 3-15　(Fig. 3-15)

Practice the above actions three times altogether.

For the 2nd and 3rd times, just repeat action 3 and action 4. At the end of the 3rd time, lay two hands at the sides of the body naturally.

(2) Action points

① Movements emphasize softness, ceaselessness, and uniform.

② Concentrate mind at Laogong point while lifting and lowering arms.

③ Movements go along with breathing. Inhale while lifting arms, and exhale while lowering them.

(3) Easy to make mistakes

① When setting feet apart, the body is off balance with limbs stiff.

② Raise and lower arms in a straight line, shrug shoulders, tilt elbows up, and turn wrist out.

(4) Functions and effects

Get rid of all stray thoughts, adjust the body to a ready position, regulate breathing and reach a quiet and tranquil mental state, and all these are preconditions to begin practice.

Exercise 1 Tiger Exercise

While practicing Tiger Exercise, try to mimic the manner of a tiger, mightiness and majesty with eyes staring ahead. Tiger Exercise is composed of two motions: Raising Tiger's Paws and Catching a Prey.

第一戏　虎戏

Raising Tiger's Paws

(1) Actions

Action 1: Move and straighten two arms forward; spread fingers and thumbs and bend them to form "tiger's paws" with palms downward, eyes on the hands (Fig. 3-16).

动作二：旋臂，由小指向拇指依次弯曲、内收，握拳；随后，两拳上提，拳心相对，两拳距离同肩宽；眼随拳走（图3-17）。两拳上提至肩前时，缓慢松拳变掌，上举至头上方；随即，撑掌变"虎爪"；眼看双手（图3-18）。

Action 2: Turn arms outward, flex fingers and thumbs one by one from little finger to thumb to make fists, and then raise both fists along the front sides of the body to the level of shoulders, thumb to thumb. Eyes follow the fists (Fig. 3-17). Slowly unclench fists and change them into palms at the shoulder level, and raise palms above head and form "tiger's paws", eyes on the hands (Fig. 3-18).

图 3-16　（Fig. 3-16）　　图 3-17　（Fig. 3-17）　　图 3-18　（Fig. 3-18）

动作三：两臂外旋，手腕立起，屈指握拳，拳心相对；眼看双拳。

Action 3: Turn arms outward, bend fingers and thumbs to clench fists with thumb to thumb, erect wrists, and eyes on the fists.

动作四：两拳下拉，拳距同肩宽；至肩前时，松拳变掌（图3-19）。随后，两掌下按，停于腹前，掌心向下；目视两掌（图3-20）。

Action 4: Pull fists down to the front of shoulders keeping the same distance as shoulders, then unclench them and change them into palms (Fig. 3-19), and push palms down to the front of the abdomen with palms downward, eyes on the palms (Fig. 3-20).

本势动作上下为一遍，共做四遍。

Action 1 to Action 4 is one round of exercise. Do it four times altogether.

第二～四遍重复第一～四步动作。第四遍结束后，两手自然垂放于体侧，目视前方（图3-21）。

In the 2nd-4th rounds, just repeat action 1-4. At the end of the 4th round, lay two hands at the sides of the body naturally, looking straight ahead (Fig. 3-21).

图 3-19　（Fig. 3-19）

图 3-20　（Fig. 3-20）

图 3-21　（Fig. 3-21）

（2）动作要点

① 手型、手法变换清晰、到位、连贯。

② 两掌上托时，力达掌根，身体充分伸展；下拉时，沉肩坠肘，力贯双拳，脚趾抓地，气沉丹田。

③ 手眼配合，协调一致。

④ 配合呼吸，自然顺畅。两掌上提与下拉时吸气，上举与下按时呼气。

（3）易犯错误

① 手型、手法变换模糊不清，松与紧变换不充分。

② 身形不正。两掌上托、下拉时，身体松懈，前倾后仰。

（2）*Action points*

① It is supposed to be clear, accurate and ceaseless for hands to change their forms and gestures.

② When raising two palms, get the body fully stretched and feel like strength reaching heal of hand; when lowering them, sink shoulders and elbows and feel like the power going through fists, toes grasping the ground, leading qi down into Dantian.

③ Eyes and hands are supposed to coordinate with each other.

④ Movements go along with breathing. Inhale while raising palms and exhale while lowering them.

（3）*Easy to make mistakes*

① It is not clear enough for hands to change their forms and gestures, and is not sufficient for hands to shift between looseness and tightness.

② The body stays loose, leaning forward or backward when raising or lowering hands.

③ 两掌在上托、下拉时，距离过宽或过窄。

(4) 动作功效

① 通过两掌的上托、下按，牵拉两胁，疏通三焦，调理脏腑机能。

② 通过拳、掌、爪的变化，增强握力，刺激末梢神经，改善手三阴经、手三阳经的循环。

虎扑

(1) 动作

动作一：接前式（虎举）。两手空拳收于髋前；随后，两拳沿身体两胁向上摩运至肩上方；两膝微屈，上体微后展；眼睛看向前上方30°～45°方向（图3-22）。

图3-22　(Fig. 3-22)

动作二：两手向额上方划弧变"虎爪"；随后上体前俯，挺胸塌腰，双爪前扑，爪心向下；眼睛平视前方（图3-23）。

③ The distance between hands is either too wide or too short while raising or lowering them.

(4) Functions and effects

① By raising up and pressing down palms, flanks are stretched, circulation of qi in Sanjiao is enhanced, and functions of Zang-fu organs can be promoted.

② By shifting hand forms of fists, palms, and paws, the gripping power of hands can be strengthened, peripheral nerves can be stimulated, and blood circulations in Hand Three Yin Meridians and Hand Three Yang Meridians can be improved.

Catching a Prey

(1) Actions

Action 1: Continue with the last move of "Raising Tiger's Paws". Clench hollow fists and rest them at each side of the abdomen, and move them up against each flank of the body to the level of shoulders while bending knees slightly and extending the upper body backward slightly; look up about 30-45 degrees (Fig. 3-22).

图3-23　(Fig. 3-23)

Action 2: Reach out both fists upward and then forward in an arc line, and then change fists into "tiger's paws" with palms downward; meanwhile, bend up-

动作三：屈膝下蹲，松腰敛臀，上体坐立；同时，沉肩收臂于两膝外侧爪心向下，力达掌根；眼睛看向前下方（图3-24）。挺膝，送髋，展腹，起身站立，上体微后仰；同时，"虎爪"变空拳沿身体两胁向上提至肩前；目视前上方30°~45°方向（图3-25）。

Action 3: Bend knees to a squatting position with chest contracted, upper body in a sitting position, waist relaxed and hips taken in meanwhile, sink shoulders and lower both hands at the outside of knees, and shift hands form to "tiger's paws" with palms downward, and feel like power reaching heel of palms; look forward below (Fig. 3-24). Move both knees and hips forward, bend upper body backward, and reach abdomen out forward; meanwhile, change hands form from "tiger's paws" to hollow fists, and raise them to the shoulder level along the flank of the body; look up about 30-45 degrees (Fig. 3-25).

图 3-24　（Fig. 3-24）

(a)　　　　　(b)

图 3-25　（Fig. 3-25）

动作四：右脚脚尖外展约30°，左腿屈膝抬起后向前落步，脚跟着地成左虚步；同时，两臂划弧上举变"虎爪"后，上体前倾，两"虎爪"向前下扑出，至大腿两侧，爪心向下；眼睛看向前下方（图3-26、图3-27）。上体抬起，左脚收回，两脚还原成水平状，自然站立；两手自然垂收于身体两侧；眼睛平视前方（图3-28）。

Action 4: Turn right foot outward about 30 degrees, bend and lift left knee and move one step forward with heel on the ground forming a left empty stance; meanwhile, raise fists up in an arc line and shift them into "tiger's paws", and then push them forward and downward to the sides of knees with palms down; look front below. (Fig. 3-26, Fig. 3-27). Lift upper body and withdraw left leg, stand with feet apart; two hands drop at the sides of the body naturally; look straight ahead (Fig. 3-28).

图 3-26 （Fig. 3-26） 图 3-27 （Fig. 3-27） 图 3-28 （Fig. 3-28）

动作五～动作八：同第一～四动作，但左右相反。

本势动作左右为一遍，共做两遍。

第二遍结束后，做一次调息动作。方法：两掌经身体两侧45°方向向上举起，掌心斜向上，至与胸同高时，屈肘，内合，下按；眼睛平视前方（图3-29、图3-30）。

Action 5-8：is the same as action 1-4，but reverse left and right.

Action 1 to Action 4 is one round of exercise. Do it twice.

At the end of the 2nd round，regulate breathing once. Method：raise both palms to the level of the chest with palms tilted up，keeping 45 degrees between body and arms，then bend elbows，draw palms close，press them down and lay them at the sides of the body naturally； look straight.（Fig. 3-29，Fig. 3-30）.

图 3-29 （Fig. 3-29） 图 3-30 （Fig. 3-30）

（2）动作要点

① 虎扑前伸时，引腰向前水平拉伸，牵拉脊柱，节节打开；两臂用力前伸，手腕放平，力达两爪；两膝蹬直，臀部向后加力。

② 动作三中，屈膝下蹲要配合含胸收腹，两手回收，宽度为两肩半回落位置在膝前、脚后，约与腰同高。

③ 展体时，要按照由下向上的顺序连贯完成，即伸膝—送髋—挺腹—后仰，以脊柱带动四肢动作。

（3）易犯错误

① 伸展不够充分，前伸时，猫腰、弯膝、屈肘。

② 虎扑提膝、落脚时，身体重心不稳或偏离。

③ 躯干动作不够圆活、连贯，或僵硬、呆板，或松懈、绵软。

（4）动作功效

① 虎扑动作注重脊柱的伸展与收放，尤其是向前的水平前扑动作，力在腰间，配合塌腰、挺胸、抬头前看，将脊柱各关节拉长，提高脊柱的柔韧性和活动范围，改善腰背部疾患。

② 增强肩、背、腰、腿力量，对慢性疾病有改善作用，如肩周炎、腰肌劳损等。

(2) *Action points*

① When reaching out body with "tiger's paws", give the upper body a level stretch forward, extending spine as far as possible; stretch two arms forward to the fullest extent with wrists leveled and power reaching two hands; straighten two knees and pull hips backward to have a good stretch of spine.

② In action 3, take chest and abdomen in while bending knees to a squatting position; take hands back to the position before knees and after toes at waist height, and the distance between hands is about two and half times the width of shoulders.

③ When stretching body backward, follow this order ceaselessly: extend both knees, move hips forward, reach abdomen out forward, and bend upper body backward with spine leading limbs.

(3) *Easy to make mistakes*

① Not being able to stretch the body fully. When extending arms forward, back is arched, knees are bent, or elbows are flexed.

② When lifting knee and lowering foot on the ground in "Catching a Prey", body balance is not well maintained.

③ It is not stretchable or continuous enough for body trunk to move, being either stiff and inflexible or loose and forceless.

(4) *Functions and effects*

① "Catching a Prey" emphasizes stretching and contracting the spine, especially in giving upper body a level extension forward, power lies in the waist with back arched, chest out, head up and eyes forward to make the joints in spine flexible and stretchable and reduce malfunctions in waist and back.

② It can strengthen the muscles in shoulders, back, waist and legs, and relieve some symptoms such as lumbar muscle strain, chronic lumbar sprain.

③ 疏肝理气，畅通经络，调和气血，调理任脉与督脉。

第二戏 鹿 戏

习练鹿戏时，要模仿鹿轻盈安逸、自由奔放的神态。鹿戏由鹿抵和鹿奔两个动作组成。

鹿抵

（1）动作

动作一：屈膝微蹲，两掌变空拳；随后，重心右移，上体微右转，两经身体右侧自然上摆，拳心向下，两臂保持松沉，两拳约肩高；同时，左脚经右脚内侧向左前方约 45°上步，脚跟着地，眼睛看右拳（图 3-31）。

③ It helps to disperse and rectify the depressed liver, circulate meridians, harmonize qi and blood, and regulate Ren Channel (conception vessel) and Du Channel (governor vessel).

Exercise 2　Deer Exercise

Try to mimic the manner of deer, swiftness, peace, freedom, and unrestraint when practicing Deer Exercise. Deer Exercise consists of two motions: Colliding with Antlers and Deer Running.

第二戏 鹿戏

Colliding with Antlers

(1) *Actions*

Action 1: Bend both knees slightly, two palms turning into hollow fists; rest body weight on the right leg, turn body slightly to the right, and raise hollow fists to the shoulder level along the right side of body with fist palms down; meanwhile, move left foot to the left front about 45 degrees between the inner sides of feet, heel touching ground and eyes on the right fist (Fig. 3-31).

图 3-31　（Fig. 3-31）

动作二：身体前倾约 30°，重心落到左腿上，左膝弯曲，左脚尖外展约 90°，全脚掌着地，右腿伸直，右脚全脚掌踏地，右脚尖朝向正前方；同时，空拳变"鹿角"，带动身体、两臂向左后方平转后伸，右臂与头同高，大臂贴耳；左肘内收，轻抵左腰侧两掌心向外，指尖朝后；头左转看右脚脚跟（图 3-32）。

Action 2: Lean the body forward about 30 degrees and shift bodyweight on the left leg, bend the left knee and turn tiptoes about 90 degrees outward with sole on the ground while stretching right leg straight with sole on the ground and tiptoes facing forward; meanwhile, change hollow fists into "deer's antlers" and move them upward, leftward, and backward in an arc line to the head level with right upper arm touching the ear and palm facing outward while left elbow taken in and touching left side of waist slightly with fingertips facing backward; head turn left and eyes on the right heel (Fig. 3-32).

图 3-32　（Fig. 3-32）

动作三：立腰起身，重心落于右腿，左膝自然伸直，左脚脚尖抬起，左脚跟着地；随后，身体右转，收左脚还原至站立，两脚水平同肩宽；同时两臂松展，经头上向右下划弧，鹿角变空拳下落至两髋旁；眼睛看前下方（图 3-33）。

Action 3: Straighten the waist, switch bodyweight on the right leg while straightening left knee with tiptoes raised and heel on the ground; then turn body to the right, withdraw left foot, and stand with two feet apart, keeping the same distance as the shoulder; meanwhile, stretch both arms and move them upward, rightward, and then downward in an arc line, changing "deer's antlers" into hollow fists and lowering them beside the hips of body; look front below (Fig. 3-33).

动作四～动作六：同动作一～三，但左右相反。

Action 4-6 is to repeat action 1-3, but reverse left and right.

图 3-33 (Fig. 3-33)

本势动作左右为一遍,共做两遍。

第二遍结束后,两手自然垂放于体侧,眼睛平视前方。

(2)动作要点

① 腰部左右旋转时,与上步方向同侧的手臂,通过肘抵靠腰部动作有意识地加力挤压;另一侧手臂(上臂)借助腰部的拧转充分后伸,使大臂贴近头部(靠近耳侧);同时,眼睛透过同侧大臂看后脚脚跟。

② 身体前倾30°~45°,头与后脚脚跟成一条直线;后脚踏实朝向正前,以固定下肢,加大腰腹部的拧转幅度,运转尾闾。

③ 动作配合呼吸,两臂上提时吸气,水平后伸时呼气。

(3)易犯错误

① 前倾时,身体弯曲过大或后仰,

Action 1 to action 6 is one round of exercise. Do it twice.

At the end of the 2nd round, lay two hands at the sides of the body naturally, looking straight ahead.

(2) Action points

① While bending and turning waist, contract the bent side of the waist with the elbow of that side pressing against the bent waist consciously; meanwhile, the other arm is fully stretched backward with upper arm keeping close to the head; look at the heel of the back foot over the upper arm of the same side.

② Lean body forward about 30-45 degrees, keeping head in a line with the rear heel; set the rear foot still with toes pointing to the front to stabilize the leg; widen the twisting range of waist and abdomen, exercising Weilyu (the coccygeal vertebrae) in mind.

③ Movements go along with breathing. Inhale while raising arms up, and exhale while stretching the body backward.

(3) Easy to make mistakes

① When leaning forward, bend too much or lean

未拔长；上步角度过大或过小；后脚脚跟离地，膝关节弯曲。

② 身体侧屈不充分，颈部不动，眼睛未看后脚脚跟。

（4）动作功效

① 提高脊柱及腰部的灵活性，增强腰部肌肉力量，防治腰部脂肪沉积、腰椎小关节紊乱等症。

② 中医有"腰为肾之府"之说，意思是人体的肾脏位于腰部，腰是肾的家、归宿。锻炼、保养腰部是调理肾脏功能最有效、最直接的办法。鹿戏是针对腰部也就是肾脏的专门运动，长期练习可起到强腰补肾强筋健骨的功效。

鹿奔

（1）动作

动作一：左腿屈膝上提，左脚尖勾起，前跨一步，落步屈膝成左弓步，右膝伸直；同时，两手握空拳经两胁上提，向斜上方划弧后落至肩前，松腕沉肘，两臂微弯，拳心向下；眼睛平视前方（图3-34）。

动作二：重心后坐至右腿，右膝弯曲，臀部与右脚脚跟上下垂直，左膝自然伸直，全脚掌着地；同时，低头顶背，含胸收腹，松腰敛臀；两臂内旋前伸，两掌变"鹿角"，掌背相对，两腕相距两拳宽（图3-35）。

backward, or not stretch out enough; the angle between two feet when stepping forward is either too big or too small; the rear heel is taken off the ground and the knee is bent.

② It is not enough for the waist to twist sideward or the neck keeps still so not be able to see the rear heel.

（4）*Functions and effects*

① Enhance the flexibility of the spine and the waist, strengthen the muscles in the waist, and prevent storing fat in the waist and derangement in the small joints of lumbar vertebrae, and etc.

② In TCM it is believed that "Waist is the home of kidneys". So the best and most effective way of improving the function of kidneys is to take good care of the waist. Deer Exercise is devised just for the waist and kidneys and if one can insist on practicing, the waist can be strengthened functions of kidneys can be improved, and muscles and bones can be built up.

Deer Running

（1）*Actions*

Action 1: Lift left knee with tiptoes upward, and then take one step forward and make a left bow stance while stretching right leg straight; meanwhile, lift hollow fists upward and forward in an arc line along flanks to the shoulder level with shoulder-width apart, both arms bent slightly, wrists relaxed and elbows sunk with fists downward; look straight ahead (Fig. 3-34).

Action 2: Rest body weight on right leg with right knee bent and hips and right heel in a line, while stretching left knee straight with sole on the ground; meanwhile, lower head, arch back, draw chest in slightly, contract abdomen, and relax waist and take in hips; turn both arms inward, form "deer's antlers" with both hands, and reach them out forward with hand backs facing each other and keeping about two-fists apart (Fig. 3-35).

图 3-34　(Fig. 3-34)

(a)　　　　　(b)

图 3-35　(Fig. 3-35)

动作三：上体抬起，还原成左弓步；松肩沉肘，两臂外旋，"鹿角"变空拳，松腕沉肘，腕同肩高，拳心向下；眼睛平视前方（图3-36）。

Action 3: Raise upper body and restore left bow stance while stretching right leg straight; relax shoulders and sink wrists, turn both arms outward, and change "deer's antlers" into hollow fists with fist palms downward at the shoulder level, relaxing wrists and sinking elbows; look straight ahead (Fig. 3-36).

动作四：收左脚成开立步；松拳变掌收于体侧；眼睛平视前方（图3-37）。

Action 4: Take back left foot and stand straight with feet apart; unclench fists into palms and lower them at the sides of the body; look straight ahead (Fig. 3-37).

图 3-36　(Fig. 3-36)

图 3-37　(Fig. 3-37)

动作五～动作八：同动作一～动作四，但左右相反。

本势动作左右为一遍，共做两遍。

第二遍结束后，做一次调息动作。方法：两掌经身体两侧45°方向向上举起，掌心斜向上，至与胸同高时，屈肘，内合，下按；眼睛平视前方（图3-38、图3-39）。

Action 5-8 is to repeat action 1-4, but reverse left and right.

Action 1 to action 8 is one round of exercise. Do it twice.

At the end of the 2nd round, regulate breathing once. Method: raise both palms forward to the level of the chest with palms tilted up, keeping 45 degrees between body and arms, and then bend elbows, draw palms close, press them down, and lay them at the sides of the body naturally; look straight ahead (Fig. 3-38, Fig. 3-39).

图 3-38　(Fig. 3-38)

图 3-39　(Fig. 3-39)

（2）动作要点

① 提腿跨步要有弧度，抬腿高度平于髋部；跨大步落小步，落步时要轻灵，体现鹿的灵巧和安舒。

② 后坐时，形成"横""竖"两张弓。"横弓"动作在背部，做到两臂水平前伸，胸部内含，舒展肩胛；"竖弓"动作在躯干，做到头前伸，背部后拱，腹收缩，臀内敛。大椎向前向下扣，胸贴背，腹贴腰，两臂夹住耳侧；尾闾向

（2）*Action points*

① When taking one step forward, lift the leg to the level of hips in an arch line, make a big step in the air, but a half step on the ground gently to show the swift and calm manner of deer.

② When body weight is rested on the back leg, form two bows, a "horizontal bow" and a "vertical bow"; the "horizontal bow" appears when extending both arms forward with chest in and shoulder blades spread open; the "vertical bow" appears when head stretching forward with back arched, abdomen contract-

前向上扣，突出命门，拉伸督脉。

③ 配合呼吸练习。提膝跨步时吸气，落脚弓步时呼气；身体重心后坐时吸气，还原弓步时呼气。

(3) 易犯错误

① 弓步动作两脚前后成一条线，重心不稳；后坐时，身体未完全落于后腿，前脚脚尖抬起，前膝弯曲或翘臀、塌腰，上体歪斜。

② 脊柱变化不明显，未形成"横弓"与"竖弓"。

(4) 动作功效

① "横弓"动作可充分舒展肩、背部肌肉、筋骨，促进血液循环，改善肩颈部位的慢性疾病或退行性病变；"竖弓"动作通过躯干的纵向开合，矫正脊柱不良弯曲，增强腰、背部肌肉力量。

② 该动作能有效提升人体督脉经气，振奋全身的阳气。

第三戏 熊 戏

习练熊戏时，要模仿熊憨厚沉稳、笨中显灵的神态。熊戏由熊运和熊晃两个动作组成。

ed, and hips held up. Dazhui bends forward and downward, chest and abdomen fully contracted to push the back, both arms keeping close to the ears; lift Weilyu upward and forward, protruding Mingmen to stretch Du Channel.

③ Movements go along with breathing. Inhale while lifting knee and exhale while making a bow stance; inhale while sitting back, and exhale while restoring a bow stance.

(3) *Easy to make mistakes*

① When putting down the foot, two feet are kept in one straight line, resulting in off-balance; when sitting back, bodyweight is not totally on the back leg, front tiptoes tilted, front knee bent, hips held up and waist relaxed, resulting in the misshaping upper body.

② It is not obvious to form a "horizontal bow" and a "vertical bow".

(4) *Functions and effects*

① Horizontal bow can fully stretch the muscles and bones in shoulders and back so that the blood circulation can be improved, the syndromes or degenerative changes in neck and shoulders can be relieved; "vertical bow" can help to correct the spinal deformity, and build up the muscles in back and waist by expanding and contracting upper body vertically.

② Help to better circulate qi in Du Channel and inspire Yangqi in the whole body.

Exercise 3 Bear Exercise

The manner of composure, peace, dexterity as well as heaviness of a bear is supposed to be manifested when practicing Bear Exercise. Bear Exercise is composed of two motions: Bear Rotating and Bear Swaying.

| 熊运 | Bear Rotating |

（1）动作 / (1) Actions

第三戏 熊戏

动作一：松膝沉髋微蹲，两掌变"熊掌"手型上提至小腹部，两腕轻贴小腹，拳眼相对，眼看"熊掌"（图3-40）。

Action 1: Squat slightly with knees relaxed and hips sunk, and change palms into "bear paws" and lift them above the abdomen, wrists touching abdomen slightly and thumbs facing each other, eyes on the fists (Fig. 3-40).

图3-40　(Fig. 3-40)

图3-41　(Fig. 3-41)

图3-42　(Fig. 3-42)

动作二：髋关节以下保持不动，腰、腹带动上体由右向左划立圆摇晃；同时，两"熊掌"以肚脐为中心，自正下向右上、正上、左下、正下方向顺势划圆，连续两圈；眼睛随上体摇晃环视地面（图3-41至图3-44）。

Action 2: Take waist as an axis to rotate upper body clockwise while body below hips keeping motionless, and make two clockwise circles continuously meanwhile, take navel as the center and move "bear's paws" in a circle along under, right above, up, left below and down for two circles; eyes follow the ground with rotating of upper body (Fig. 3-41 to Fig. 3-44).

动作三、四：同动作一、二，唯方向相反。

Action 3, 4: repeat action 1, action 2, but reverse left and right.

本势为原地定式动作，下肢不动，上体按照先顺（右）后逆（左）的顺序各摇晃两圈。

Keep legs still and rotate upper body clockwise for two circles first, and then anticlockwise for another two circles.

图 3-43 （Fig. 3-43）　　图 3-44　（Fig. 3-44）　　图 3-45　（Fig. 3-45）

逆时针摇晃结束后，两手自然垂放于体侧，眼睛平视前方（图 3-45）。

After the last rotating, unclench fists and lay them at the sides of the body naturally, looking straight ahead（Fig. 3-45）.

（2）动作要点

① "两个不动"。松腰、实腹、坐髋，摇晃时保持髋关节不动；两臂松沉收于下腹部，两拳相距约一拳宽，拳眼相对，手指朝下，两臂保持不动。

② 上体摇晃时，两拳因腰、腹部的摇晃做被动摩运，手腕部轻贴腹部，以神阙（肚脐）为中心，经丹田（下）、章门（左右）、中脘（上）划圆，协调自然。

③ 外导与内引相互作用。掌划立圆为外导，摇晃腰腹为内引，意念存于下丹田。

（2）Action points

① " Two motionless". When rotating upper body, keep hip joints still, with waist relaxed, abdomen kept solid and hips fallen down; keep two arms still when rotating, with two arms relaxed and sunk, fists laid on the underbelly, thumbs facing each other and keeping a fist-width, and fingers pointing downward.

② When rotating upper body, two fists are moved along the rotating of waist and abdomen with wrists touching abdomen slightly Fists are moved to make a circle along the points of Dantian（down）, Zhangmen（left and right）and Zhongwan（up）, taking Shenque（navel）as the center.

③ Interaction is created between leading-in by moving "bears paws" on belly and leading-out by swaying waist and abdomen. Warmth can be produced and led into the body by moving "bear's paws" on belly, and warmth can also be produced and led out of the body by swaying waist and abdomen, mind concentrating at Lower Dantian.

④ 呼吸配合。一吸一呼为一圈，先吸后呼。

（3）易犯错误

① 两掌主动划圆或不动。

② 膝、胯、腰等关节晃动，出现身体的前倾、后仰和左右转体。

③ 目光平视或仰视，未跟随身体进行移动。

（4）动作功效

① 摇晃上体，起到调理中焦、加强脾胃运化的作用。

② 防治人体慢性损伤，如腰肌劳损、软组织损伤；通过腰腹摇晃，可改善消化不良、食欲不振、便秘、腹泻等病症。

熊晃

（1）动作

动作一：起身站立，以右腿为支撑，左髋关节主动上提，左脚离地；左膝、踝放松，自然微屈；两臂自然下垂，手型为"熊掌"；眼睛平视左前方（图3-46）。

动作二：向身体左前方45°上步，落髋，脚尖朝正前，成左弓步；同时，左肩顺势前靠，左臂内旋前摆至左膝前上方，拳心向外；右拳内旋后摆至右髋高度，拳心向后；视线沿左拳方向自然前看（图3-47）。

④ Coordinate inhale and exhale. One inhaling and one exhaling is a circle Inhale first then exhale.

(3) Easy to make mistakes

① Two fists take the initiative to make a circle or keep motionless.

② Too excessive body rotating, such as rotating joints of knees, hips, and waist, or body leaning forward and backward, or swaying leftward and Rightward.

③ Looking forward or upward, eyes fail to follow the rotating of the upper body.

(4) Functions and effects

① When rotating the upper body, the function of Middle Jiao can be regulated, and transformation and transportation of spleen and stomach can be strengthened.

② Help to prevent chronic injuries such as lumbar muscle, and soft tissue injury. In addition, rotating waist and abdomen can have some effects on indigestion, poor appetite, constipation, and diarrhea.

Bear Swaying

(1) Actions

Action 1: Shift body weight to the right leg and lift the left foot from the ground by raising left hip, slightly flexing left knee and ankle; make the form of "bears paws" with two hands and rest them at the sides of the body; look straight left front (Fig. 3-46).

Action 2: Shift body weight left forward about 45 degrees and make a left bow stance with tiptoes pointing forward; meanwhile, turn left shoulder inward and extend left arm forward above left knee with fist palm facing left; turn the right fist inward and move it back to the hip level with palm facing backward and look ahead (Fig. 3-47).

图 3-46 (Fig. 3-46)

图 3-47 (Fig. 3-47)

动作三：沉髋后坐，身体左转，右膝弯曲，左膝自然伸直；以腰带背、臂做前后的弧形摆动；眼睛随身体转动自然平视（图 3-48）。

Action 3: Turn body left and shift body weight backward by flexing right knee and straightening left knee naturally; sway body with arms forward and backward in an arc line, waist leading shoulders and arms forward and backward in an arc line, look forward with the swaying body (Fig. 3-48).

图 3-48 (Fig. 3-48)

图 3-49 (Fig. 3-49)

动作四：身体右转，重心前移，左腿屈膝，右腿伸直；同时，左臂内旋前靠，

Action 4: Turn body from left to right, and shift bodyweight forward by flexing the left leg and stretc-

第三章 健身气功·五禽戏动作图解 51

左拳摆至左膝前上方，拳心向左，右拳摆至体后，拳心向后；目视左前方（图3-49）。

动作五～动作八：同动作一至动作四，唯左右相反。

本势动作左右为一遍，共做两遍。

第二遍结束后，做一次调息动作。方法：两掌经身体两侧45°方向向上举起，掌心斜向上，至与胸同高时，屈肘，内合，下按；眼睛平视前方（图3-50至图3-52）。

hing the right leg; meanwhile, turn the left arm inward and move it forward with fist above the knee and fist palm facing left, while moving the right fist backward behind the body with palm facing backward; look left front (Fig. 3-49).

Action 5-8 is to repeat action 1-4, but reverse left and right.

Action 1 to action 8 is one round of exercise. Do it twice.

At the end of the 2nd round, regulate breathing once. Method: raise both palms forward to the chest level with palms tilted up, keeping 45 degrees between body and arms; then bend elbows, draw palms close, press them down and lay them at the sides of the body naturally; look straight ahead (Fig. 3-50 to Fig. 3-52).

图 3-50　（Fig. 3-50）

图 3-51　（Fig. 3-51）

图 3-52　（Fig. 3-52）

（2）动作要点

① 上步动作，核心力量在腰腹部，以腰侧收缩带动髋部的上提与下沉落步时，前脚掌要全脚踏地，松腰沉髋，弓步后腿自然伸直。

（2）Action points

① When moving a step forward, strength lies in waist and abdomen, raising hips up and down by contracting the lateral group of lumbar muscles. When making a bow stance, flex the front knee with the sole of the foot on the ground while stretching the

② 上步脚脚尖朝正前，落步后两脚横向间距稍宽于肩，成弓步步型；以腰带动肩、背、手臂的运摆；上下肢协调一致。

（3）易犯错误

① 腰侧未收紧，髋关节没有上提动作或上提不充分，形成屈膝抬腿，主动向下伸膝落步，落步后，前腿僵直，后腿弯曲，未成弓步。

② 前脚脚尖外撇或内扣，重心移动时，上体前俯后仰。

③ 上体不动，两臂做前后摆臂动作，没有内、外旋转。

（4）动作功效

① 通过提髋、落步、转体、摆臂，反复刺激与摩运人体脏腑器官，对肝、脾有特殊疗效，起到疏肝理气、调理脾胃的作用。

② 加强髂腰肌力量，提高髋关节周围肌肉的力量与活动范围。对老年人下肢无力、髋关节损伤、膝痛有改善作用。

第四戏 猿戏

习练猿戏时，要模仿猿的轻灵敏捷、左顾右盼的天性。猿戏由猿提和猿摘两个动作组成。

back leg naturally, waist relaxed and hips sunk.

② Step forward with tiptoes pointing forward, and make a bow stance with a little wider-than-shoulder distance between two feet. Take the waist as an axis and sway the upper body with shoulders and arms. Upper and lower limbs keep in step with each other.

（3） *Easy to make mistakes*

① When turning body sideways, not twist waist enough, or not have a lift of hips or not lift enough so that front knee is bent. When making a bow stance, the front leg keeps straight and the back leg is bent.

② When stepping forward, front tiptoes turn inward or outward; when shifting bodyweight, the upper body leans forward and backward.

③ The upper body keeps motionless, two arms swaying forward and backward without turning inward or outward.

（4） *Functions and effects*

① By lifting hips, stepping down on the ground, turning body left and right, and swaying two arms, Zang-fu organs are stimulated and massaged, the functions of liver and spleen can be promoted, stagnated liver qi can be dispersed, and liver and spleen are harmonized.

② It can strengthen the muscles of the iliopsoas and hip joints, and enlarge the range of activity of hip joints. In addition, it can alleviate the symptoms such as weakness of lower limbs for the aging people, hip joints injuries and pains in knee joints.

Exercise 4　Monkey Exercise

When practicing Monkey Exercise, try to mimic the manner of a monkey, agility, and quickness, and nature of glancing around. Monkey Exercise is composed of two motions: Monkey Lifting and Monkey Picking.

第四戏　猿戏

| 猿提 | Monkey Lifting |

（1）动作

动作一：体前出掌，十指撑开，随即屈腕搓拢成"猿钩"（图3-53、图3-54）。

(1) Actions

Action 1: Put two hands forward, extend ten fingers and separate them from one another, and then bend wrists and collect fingers together forming "monkey's hooked paws" (Fig. 3-53, Fig. 3-54).

图3-53 (Fig. 3-53)

图3-54 (Fig. 3-54)

动作二：耸肩缩颈，两臂内裹，立腰收腹，提肛；两手腕上领提至胸前，大小臂夹紧；同时上提脚跟，头左转，眼睛平视左方向（图3-55）。

Action 2: Lift two hands to the chest level, shrug shoulders, clamp arms, erect waist, contract abdomen, and clench anus; meanwhile, lift up heels and turn head to the left, and look directly to the left (Fig. 3-55).

动作三：转头回正，松肩落臂，松腹落肛，松钩变掌，指尖相对，掌心向下，眼睛平视正前方（图3-56）。

Action 3: Turn head to the front position, relaxing shoulders, arms, abdomen, and anus; change the form of hands from "monkeys hooked paws to palms with fingertips facing each other and palms downward; look straight ahead (Fig. 3-56).

动作四：松臂落掌回于体侧，脚跟回落，全脚掌着地；眼睛平视正前方（图3-57）。

Action 4: Relax arms and put palms down at the sides of the body, put heels back with soles on the ground; look straight ahead (Fig. 3-57).

动作五～动作八：同动作一～动作四，唯头向右转。

Action 5-8 is to repeat action 1-4, with head turning to the right side.

(a)

(b)

图 3-55 （Fig. 3-55）

图 3-56 （Fig. 3-56）

图 3-57 （Fig. 3-57）

本势动作左右为一遍，共做两遍。

第二遍结束后，两手自然垂放于体侧，眼睛平视正前方。

(2) 动作要点

① 掌变"猿钩"时，迅速搓拢，

Action 1 to action 8 is one round of exercise. Do it twice.

At the end of the 2nd round, lay two hands at the sides of the body naturally, looking straight ahead.

(2) *Action points*

① It should be quick to change the form of hands

第三章　健身气功·五禽戏动作图解　55

五指自然捏拢。

②上提动作遵循耸肩—收腹—提肛—脚跟离地—转头的顺序。

③"五升一降"。升，百会领带身体重心向上，肩、腕、裆、踝上提；降，颈部向下收缩。

④"六个力"。上，重心上提；下，颈椎下降；左右，肩臂内收；前后，夹肘，手臂收于身前，团胸收腹，背部向后撑起。

⑤动作配合提肛呼吸。上提时吸气，意在会阴；下按时呼气，放下会阴部。

（3）易犯错误

①上提时，腹、臀、下肢未收紧，重心不稳，前后晃动。

②耸肩不充分，团胸、夹肘不明显。

（4）动作功效

①"猿钩"的快速变化，可提高机体反应的灵敏性。

②提踵（踝关节）直立，可增强腿部特别是踝关节的力量，提高平衡能力。

③上提与下降，可增强呼吸，按摩心脏，改善脑部供血。

from palms into "monkey's hooked paws" while five fingers holding together naturally.

② When lifting, it follows this order: shrug shoulders, contract abdomen, lift anus, raise heels off ground, and turn head.

③ "Five ascending and one descending": Five ascending refers to lifting shoulders, wrists, crotch, ankles, and center of body weight led by Baihui in mind. One descending refers to contracting neck.

④ "Six forces": up force refers to lifting body weight; downforce refers to contracting cervical vertebra; left and right forces refer to taking in shoulders and arms; front and back forces refer to folding elbows at the front body, contracting chest and abdomen, and arching backs.

⑤ Movements go along with breathing and lifting anus. When lifting, inhale with the mind at lifting Huiyin; when pressing down, exhale with the mind at relaxing Huiyin.

(3) Easy to make mistakes

① When lifting, abdomen, hips and lower limbs are loose, and the body is off-balance, leaning forward and backward.

② It is not enough to shrug shoulders, and it is not obvious to contract chest and clamp elbows.

(4) Functions and effects

① The quick-shifting of "monkey's hooked paws" helps to improve the reaction and flexibility of the body.

② Standing on tiptoes by lifting ankles can strengthen the muscles in leg and ankle joints in particular, and improve the balance ability of the body.

③ By lifting and lowering, breathing can be strengthened, heart gets massaged, and blood supply in the brain can be improved.

猿摘

(1) 动作

动作一：右腿屈膝，重心移至右腿，左脚向左后方撤步，脚尖外撇45°，脚尖点地；同时，屈左肘，左掌成"猿钩"收至腰间，合谷穴贴腰；右掌向右斜前下方自然前伸，掌心向下，眼睛随右掌伸出方向自然前看（图3-58）。

动作二：重心后移至左腿上，左脚掌着地，右脚顺势收回，落于左脚内侧，脚前掌着地，成右丁步；同时，身体左转，右臂回摆至头左侧，掌心对太阳穴；眼睛先看右掌，成丁步时，再转头看向右前上方（图3-59）。

Monkey Picking

(1) Actions

Action 1: Bend right leg and turn body weight on right leg while moving left foot left backward with tiptoes turning outward about 45 degrees and touching the ground; meanwhile, bend left elbow and form a "monkey's hooked paw" with Hegu point touching waist while stretching right arm front right side of body with palm down; eyes follow the right palm (Fig. 3-58).

Action 2: Shift body weight to left leg with sole on the ground while taking right foot into the inner side of left foot with front sole touching the ground forming a right T-stance; meanwhile, turn body left, move right arm to the left side of head with palm facing the left temple; eyes follow right palm first, when making a right T-stance, turn head and look right above (Fig. 3-59).

图3-58 （Fig. 3-58）

图3-59 （Fig. 3-59）

动作三：转右掌下按至左髋侧；眼看右掌（图3-60）。右脚向右前45°上步起身，重心前移至右腿，右膝伸直，左腿随即自然收回，左膝蹬直，左脚脚尖点

Action 3: Turn right hand and press it to the left side of hips, eyes on the right palm (Fig. 3-60). Move right foot right forward about 45 degrees and shift body weight to the right leg, straighten right knee

地；同时，右掌右上方划弧伸出，随即转体面向右45°方向，右臂横摆至右耳处提腕变"猿钩"，稍高于肩；左臂自然伸直，松钩变掌，由体后经头上向头前，提腕变"猿钩"，成采摘式；眼睛上看左手腕处（图3-61）。

while taking left leg in and straightening left knee with tiptoes touching the ground meanwhile, move right palm up in an arc line to the right ear with wrist erected and "monkey's hooked paw formed with right hand keeping a little higher than shoulders; straighten left arm and turn monkey's hooked paw?" into a palm, and move it from backward to upward and forward with wrist erected and fingertips together as if a monkey is picking fruits from a tree; eyes on the left wrist (Fig. 3-61).

图 3-60 （Fig. 3-60）

图 3-61 （Fig. 3-61）

图 3-62 （Fig. 3-62）

动作四：拇指内收，其余四指屈拢，左"猿钩"变"握固"手型；重心后坐至左腿，右脚收回，脚前掌着地，屈膝下蹲成右丁步；同时，左臂沉肩屈肘收至左肩侧，松拳变掌成托桃状，右臂伴随转体，松钩变掌，自然收至左肘下成捧托掌状（图3-62）。

Action 4: Turn "monkey's hooked paw" into a solid fist with left hand; shift body weight to left leg while taking in right foot to the side of left foot with tiptoes touching the ground to make a right T-stance; meanwhile, sink shoulder and bend elbow with left arm and move it to the left shoulder with palm facing upward and fingers separated like holding a peach while moving right palm in an arc line past front body to just below the left elbow (Fig. 3-62).

动作五～动作八：同动作一～动作四，但左右相反。

Action 5-8 is to repeat action 1-4, but reverse left and right.

本势动作左右为一遍，共做两遍。

Action 1 to action 8 is one round of exercise. Do it twice.

第二遍结束后，左脚向左横开一步，脚尖朝正前，两腿伸直，两手回至体侧，做一次调息动作。方法：两掌经身体两侧45°方向向上举起，掌心斜向上，至胸前高度，屈肘，内合，下按；眼睛平视前方（图3-63至图3-65）。

At the end of the 2nd round, move left foot a step leftward with tiptoes facing front, straighten two legs and put hands at the sides of the body, and regulate breathing once. Method: raise both palms forward to the chest level with palms tilted up, keeping 45 degrees between body and arms, then bend elbows, draw palm close, press them down and lay them at the sides of the body naturally; look straight ahead (Fig. 3-63 to Fig. 3-65).

图 3-63 （Fig. 3-63）

图 3-64 （Fig. 3-64）

图 3-65 （Fig. 3-65）

（2）动作要点

① 眼随手动，表现出猿猴的灵活与机敏。要注意上下肢的协调配合。

② 把握住猿猴的特点与特征。在后腿屈膝下蹲时，身体要团缩；蹬腿上步采摘时，身体要伸展、拉长。

③ 注意节奏的变化与劲力的收放。上步采摘时，掌变"猿钩"动作要稍加速度与力度；"猿钩"变"握固"要沉肩落臂；上手成托桃状时，掌指分开与屈蹲定势应同步。

(2) Action points

① Eyes are expected to follow the movements of arms, trying to express the swift and flexible manner of a monkey. Attentions are paid to the coordination of upper and lower limbs.

② Try to mimic the movements of monkeys. When bending knees to a squatting position, the body is contracted together; when lifting upward mimicking monkeys picking fruits, the body is supposed to be extended and stretchable.

③ Attentions are paid to the variation of rhythm and force. When mimicking monkey's picking fruits, much speed and strength are given to the switch from palms to "monkey's hooked paws"; shoulders are sunk and elbows are fallen when changing from "monkey's hooked paws" to "solid Fists"; when palm facing upward, fingers are separated like holding a peach and keep pace with the squatting position.

④ Try to mimic monkeys' manner such as looking around, alertness and flexibility, climbing trees and breaking twigs, etc.

（3）易犯错误

① 下肢动作不一致。出现手快脚慢，或手慢脚快，以及无眼神配合等问题。

② 屈膝下蹲时，身体僵直或松懈；采摘时，两腿未伸直，重心在两腿中间。

（3）Easy to make mistakes

① Lack of coordination between upper and lower limbs, such as quick hands and slow feet or vice versa, or without the cooperation of eyes.

② When bending knees in a squatting position, the body is too stiff or too relaxed; when mimicking monkeys picking fruits, keep bent legs with bodyweight in the wrong place.

（4）动作功效

① 两手在体前由手掌快速变为"猿钩"，可刺激、调节手三阴经、手三阳经的经气，增强神经、肌肉反应的灵敏性。

② 有利于颈部运动，促进和调节脑部的血液循环。

③ "提吸落呼"的呼吸方式，有助于增强心肺功能，缓解气短、气喘等症状。

（4）Functions and effects

① The quick shift between "monkey's hooked paws" and palms can stimulate and adjust qi in Hand Three Yin Meridians and Hand Three Yang Meridians, and enhance the sensibility of nerves and muscles.

② It is good for the neck and can help the blood circulation in the brain.

③ By inhaling while lifting and exhaling while lowering, the functions of the heart and lungs can be enhanced, and syndromes like shortness of breath, wheezing and so on can be relieved.

第五戏　鸟戏

第五戏　鸟戏

习练鸟戏时，要表现出鸟的轻盈身姿、优雅奔放的神韵。鸟戏由鸟伸和鸟飞两个动作组成。

Exercise 5　Bird Exercise

When practicing Bird Exercise, it is expected to manifest the manner of a bird, calmness, litheness, elegance, and unconstraint. Bird Exercise is composed of two motions: Bird Stretching and Bird Flying.

鸟伸

Bird Stretching

（1）动作

动作一：屈膝微蹲，两掌前摆，叠于腹

（1）Actions

Action 1: Take a semi-squatting position with two palms

前，左掌在上（图 3-66）。

overlapping forward, left hand on top (Fig. 3-66).

动作二：两肘自然伸直，手臂由腹前向上举起，至头前上方，大臂贴耳，提腕压指，掌心向下，指尖向前；塌腰挺胸，缩颈提肩，上体微前倾；眼睛看向前下方（图 3-67）。

Action 2: Straighten two elbows naturally and raise two hands above head with upper arms touching ears, wrists erected and fingers pressed and forward; throw out chest, contract abdomen and neck. lift shoulders, and lean upper body forward slightly; look front below (Fig. 3-67).

(a)　　　　　　(b)

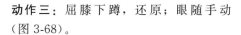

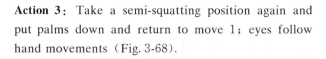

动作三：屈膝下蹲，还原；眼随手动（图 3-68）。

Action 3: Take a semi-squatting position again and put palms down and return to move 1; eyes follow hand movements (Fig. 3-68).

动作四：重心移至右腿；右膝蹬直，独立支撑，左腿伸直后摆；同时两掌分于身体两侧后向体侧后方摆起，掌心向上，手型"鸟翅"；塌腰挺胸，抬头伸颈；眼睛平视前方（图 3-69）。

Action 4: Straighten right knee and stand on the right leg while lifting and extending the left leg backward; meanwhile, spread both arms backward with palms facing up, hands in the form of "bird's wing", chest out, head up, and neck long; look straight ahead (Fig. 3-69).

动作五～动作八：同动作一～动作四，但方向相反。

Action 5-8 is to repeat action 1-4, but reverse left and right.

本势动作左右为一遍，共做两遍。

Action 1 to action 8 is one round of exercise. Do it twice.

第二遍结束后，左脚下落，两脚开步站立，两手自然垂于体侧；眼睛平视前方。

At the end of the 2nd round, put left foot down on the ground, stand straight with feet apart, lay two hands at the sides of the body, looking straight ahead.

图 3-68　(Fig. 3-68)

(a)　　　　　　　　　　(b)

图 3-69　(Fig. 3-69)

（2）动作要点

① 两掌腹前相叠，一般来说，高不过肚脐，低不过髋部，以舒适自然为宜。

② 上举时，手掌并拢，手腕微上提，手指伸直；肩、颈、腰、臀要收紧，以刺激命门、夹脊、大椎等穴；后腿摆起时，后膝伸直，后脚脚尖绷起，踝关节伸展。

③ 两臂后摆时，身体向上拔伸，脊柱呈"反弓状"；手臂与躯干成45°。

（3）易犯错误

① 平衡动作不稳，身体晃动。

② 两掌后摆时，手臂未打开或展臂角度过大。

③ 起身展体动作中，出现屈膝、折腕、耸肩。

(2) Action points

① Overlap two hands in front of the abdomen at the level between navel and hips. It is better to feel natural and comfortable.

② When raising two hands up, put palms together with wrists erected slightly and fingers straightened pointing forward; tighten shoulder, neck, waist and hips to stimulate Mingmen, Jiaji and, Dazhui; when extending back leg, straighten knee, tighten tiptoes and extend ankle joints.

③ When spreading two arms backward, stretch spine up and form a "reverse bow shape", keeping 45 degrees between arms and body.

(3) Easy to make mistakes

① The body is off balance.

② When spreading both arms backward, two arms do not spread open or spread too much.

③ When standing on one leg with arms spreading and hands in the form of "bird's wing", it is wrong to

(4) 动作功效

两臂大开大合，可扩大胸腔容积，增强肺的呼吸功能，开胸顺气，改善慢性支气管炎、哮喘、肺气肿等病症。

鸟飞

(1) 动作

动作一：屈膝下蹲，两掌合于腹前，掌心斜向上；眼睛看向前下方（图3-70）。右膝伸直，独立支撑；左腿提膝，脚尖下垂；同时，两臂伸展，体侧上摆至略高于肩，掌心向下，手型"鸟翅"；眼睛平视前方（图3-71）。

bend knee and wrists, and shrug shoulders.

(4) Functions and effects

By opening and closing two arms as far as possible, the chest is expanded and chest capacity is raised. Respiratory function of lungs can be improved and symptoms like, chronic bronchitis, asthma, and pulmonary emphysema and so on can be alleviated.

Bird Flying

(1) Actions

Action 1: Take a semi-squatting position, put two hands in front of the abdomen with palms slanting and fingertips downward, and facing each other; look front below (Fig. 3-70). Straighten right knee and stand on it, lift left knee with tiptoes pointing downward; meanwhile, raise two palms to a-little-higher-than-shoulder level with palms facing downward like a bird flying, hands in the form of "bird's wing"; look straight ahead (Fig. 3-71).

图 3-70　（Fig. 3-70）

图 3-71　（Fig. 3-71）

动作二：松膝下蹲，左脚尖点地，两腿屈蹲；同时，两掌还原腹前；眼睛看向前下方（图3-72）。

Action 2: Relax knees in a semi-squatting position with left tiptoes touching on the ground; meanwhile, return two palms to the front of the abdomen; look front below. (Fig. 3-72)

动作三：右膝伸直，独立支撑；左腿提膝，脚尖下垂；同时，两臂伸展，体侧上摆至头顶上方，掌背相对，指尖向上；眼睛平视前方（图3-73）。

Action 3: Straighten right knee and stand on it while lifting left knee with tiptoes pointing downward; meanwhile, raise two palms overhead top with palm backs facing each other and fingers pointing upward; look straight ahead (Fig. 3-73).

图 3-72 （Fig. 3-72）

图 3-73 （Fig. 3-73）

图 3-74 （Fig. 3-74）

动作四：松膝下蹲，左脚着地还原，两腿屈蹲；同时，两掌还原腹前；眼睛看向前下方（图3-74）。

Action 4: Put the left foot on the ground, bend two knees and take a semi squatting position; meanwhile, return two palms to the front position; look front below (Fig. 3-74).

动作五～动作八：同动作一～动作四，但方向相反。

Action 5-8 is to repeat action 1-4, but reverse left and right.

本势动作左右为一遍，共做两遍。

Action 1 to action 8 is one round of exercise. Do it twice.

第二遍结束后，起身站立，两脚尖朝正前，掌回体侧，做一次调息动作。方法：两掌经身体两侧45°方向向上举起，掌心斜向上，至与胸同高时，屈肘、内合、下按；眼睛平视前方（图3-75至图3-77）。

At the end of the second round, stand straight with two tiptoes facing forward, two hands return to the sides of the body and regulate breathing once. Method: raise both palms forward to the chest level with palms tilted up, keeping 45 degrees between body and arms, then bend elbows, draw palm close, press them down and lay them at the sides of the body naturally; look straight ahead (Fig. 3-75 to Fig. 3-77).

图 3-75　(Fig. 3-75)　　图 3-76　(Fig. 3-76)　　图 3-77　(Fig. 3-77)

（2）动作要点

① 两臂侧摆与上摆时，松肩沉肘，以根节（肩）带动梢节（腕指），动作舒展大方。

② 手脚同起同落，左右对称；单腿支撑时脚趾抓地，百会上领，保持身体平衡。

③ 配合呼吸，上举时吸气，回落时呼气。

（3）易犯错误

① 两臂摆动时过于僵直或松懈。

② 平衡动作重心不稳，提膝时脚踝过紧或勾起；身体前倾后仰。

③ 手型变化不明显。

（4）动作功效

① 开胸顺气，强心健肺，提高血液含氧量及交换能力。

(2) *Action points*

① When raising two hands sideward and upward, relax shoulders and sink elbows, shoulders leading elbows and fingers. Movements are supposed to be stretchable and elegant.

② Hands and feet are supposed to keep pace with one another and keep bilateral symmetry. Stand on one leg with toes grasping the ground, keeping a balanced body with Bai Hui leading up in mind.

③ Movements go along with breathing. Inhale while raising hands and exhale while lowering them.

(3) *Easy to make mistakes*

① It is too stiff or loose for two arms to move.

② The body is off balance, leaning forward or backward. When lifting knees ankles are too tight or kept in a hooked position.

③ It is not obvious for hands to change their forms.

(4) *Functions and effects*

① It helps expand the chest and circulate qi to flow, strengthen heart and lungs, and increase oxygen con-

② 鸟翅手型中，要求意念在拇指、食指上，可起到刺激手太阴肺经及加强肺经经气流通的作用。

③ 单腿提膝独立动作，可显著增强腰腹、下肢力量，提高人体平衡能力。

收势　引气归元

（1）动作

收势　引气归元

动作一：两掌侧上举，至头顶上方，意念在掌心（图3-78）。

动作二：两掌于体前下按至腹前；眼睛平视前方（图3-79）。

重复动作一、动作二2遍。

② When making "bird's wing" with hands, concentrate the mind on thumbs and index fingers to stimulate Hand Taiyin Lung Meridian and circulate qi flow in lung meridians.

③ By practicing standing on one leg with lifting another knee often, muscles in the waist, abdomen and lower limbs can be strengthened and the body balance can be improved.

Closing Position Leading Qi to Dantian

（1）Actions

Action 1：Raise two palms up above head top with two arms a little curved, concentrating mind on palm centers (Fig. 3-78).

Action 2：Press down two palms to front of the abdomen with palms downward; look straight ahead (Fig. 3-79).

Repeat action 1, action 2 twice.

图 3-78　(Fig. 3-78)

图 3-79　(Fig. 3-79)

动作三：两臂侧拉，体前划平弧，旋臂内收，掌心相对，与肚脐同高；眼睛平视前方（图 3-80）。

Action 3: Pull out two arms a little bit and make flat arcs, then turn two palms outside facing each other, at the height of front navel; look straight ahead (Fig. 3-80).

动作四：虎口交叉，并指叠掌；双目微闭，调息静养，意守丹田（图 3-81）。

Action 4: Overlap two palms with thumbs crossing each other and fingers together, half-close eyes and regulate breathing for a while concentrate mind at Dantian (Fig. 3-81).

动作五：保持双目微闭状，静养片刻后，合掌搓热（图 3-82）。

Action 5: Keep eyes half closed, and have a rest for a while. and then rub palms till warm is produced (Fig. 3-82).

图 3-80　(Fig. 3-80)

图 3-81　(Fig. 3-81)

图 3-82　(Fig. 3-82)

动作六：两掌轻贴面部，由下颌向上、外、下摩运，浴面 3 遍（图 3-83）。

Action 6: Then put palms on the face, rubbing in a semi-circle on the face starting from the lower jaw to up, outside and down three times (Fig. 3-83).

动作七：两掌经上额头向后以头顶、耳后、胸前顺序摩运下落，自然垂于体侧；同时，缓慢睁开眼睛，平视前方（图 3-84）。

Action 7: Move two palms backward along forehead, head top, back ears front chest, and finally to the sides of the body; meanwhile, open eyes slowly and look straight ahead (Fig. 3-84).

动作八：收左脚，并步，恢复成预备势动作。全套结束（图 3-85）。

Action 8: Move left foot next to right foot, return to the ready position and look ahead. The whole set of exercises is over (Fig. 3-85).

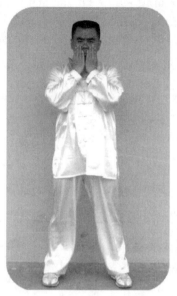
图 3-83　（Fig. 3-83）

图 3-84　（Fig. 3-84）

图 3-85　（Fig. 3-85）

（2）动作要点

① 动作配合呼吸和意念。上托时吸气，意在劳宫；下按时呼气，身体各部位松沉，意达脚底涌泉。

② 两掌合抱拢气动作，手臂先内旋再外旋，意将气息回收于丹田；动作自然流畅。

（3）易犯错误

① 两臂运行速度过快或过慢。

② 动作僵硬，手臂无旋动。

（4）动作功效

① 通过搓手、浴面，恢复常态。

② 收气静养，培补元气。

（2）*Action points*

① Movements go along with breathing and mental focus. Inhale while raising up, mind at Laogong point, and exhale while pressing down, mind at Yongquan point, all parts of the body relaxed and sunk.

② When turning two palms outside and then closing them together to the front of navel, qi is led into Dantian. Do it naturally and smoothly.

（3）*Easy to make mistakes*

① It is too fast or too slow for arms to move.

② It is too stiff for arms to make a turn or not to make any turns.

（4）*Functions and effects*

① By rubbing hands and face for a while, the normal state is restored.

② Lead qi into Dantian and take a rest for a while to replenish Congenital Qi.

健身气功·五禽戏
全套演练

第四章　太极拳概述
Chapter 4　Summary of Taiji Quan

太极拳概述

本章要点：太极拳作为中华民族传统体育项目，具有鲜明的时代特征和广泛的群众基础，在全民健身活动与对外文化交流中均发挥着不可替代的作用。本章主要讲述太极拳的源起、发展及演变，并对武德与武礼的含义与作用进行了阐述。

Key points：China Shadow Boxing, as one of the Chinese traditional sport events, has outstanding characteristics and extensive mass base, and plays an irreplaceable role in the national fitness activities and international cultural exchange. The chapter mainly introduces its origin, development, and evolution, and expounds on the implication of martial moralities and manners.

第一节　太极拳简史

太极拳是一种柔和、缓慢、轻灵的拳术。其动作轻柔圆活，处处带有弧形，运动连绵不断，势势相连。

太极拳这个名称是因为拳法变幻无穷，遂用中国古代的"阴阳""太极"这一哲学理论来解释拳理而命名的。"太极"一词源出《周易》："易有太极，是生两仪。""太"就是大的意思，"极"就是开始或顶点的意思。太极是中国古代人的一种最原始的世界观。拳术和太极相结合，逐步形成了太极拳术。

关于太极拳的起源，据考是于明末清初逐渐形成的。太极拳的来源有以下

Section 1　A Brief History of Taiji Quan

Taiji Quan is a soft, slow and light boxing It's continuous, circular and fluent movements.

Taiji Quan comes from Chinese ancient philosophy "Yin-Yang" and "Tai Ji", because of its tremendously changeable movements. The word "Taiji" comes from *Zhouyi*："Yi has Taiji（supreme terminus）, and it produces two Yi（ultimate element）"."Tai'" means supreme, and "ji" means the initial beginning or ultimate terminus or vertex. Taiji is ancient chinese primitive world view. Taiji Quan gradually came into being from the integration of Quan（boxing） skills and the theory of Taiji.

According to the original and textual researches of Taiji Quan that it is gradually formed in the late Ming

三个方面：

① 综合吸收了明代名家拳法。明代武术极为盛行，出现了很多名家、专著和新拳种，太极拳就是吸取了当时各家拳法之长，特别是戚继光的三十二势长拳而编成的。

② 结合了古代导引、吐纳之术。太极拳讲究意念引导动作，气沉丹田，心静体松，重在内壮，把拳术中的手、眼、身、步的协调配合与导引、吐纳有机地结合起来，这就使太极拳成为内外统一的拳术运动，所以被称为"内功拳"之一。

③ 运用了中国古代的中医经络学说和阴阳学说。太极拳结合经络学说，要求"以意引气，以气运身"，内气发源于丹田，以腰为主宰发力于全身。各式传统太极拳也皆以太极阴阳学说来概括和解释拳法中各种矛盾变化。

随着历史的发展，武术逐渐从战场搏杀转为体育健身，太极拳也是如此。100多年前，太极拳家在《十三势行功歌》中就有"详推用意终何在，益寿延年不老春"的提法。太极拳经过长期流传，演变出许多流派，其中流传较广或特点较显著的有陈式、杨式、武式、吴式、孙式五派。

陈式：陈式太极拳分老架与新架两

Dynasty and early Qing Dynasty. There are three aspects of Taiji Quan's origin：

① Integration of famous Quan（boxing）skills in the Ming Dynasty. It appeared many famous masters, monographs and new types of Quans when wushu was quite popular in the Ming Dynasty. Taiji Quan absorbed merits from different schools of Wushu, especially the 32Style Chang Quan invented by Qi Jiguang.

② Integrated with ancient skill breathing and inner guiding, Taiji Quan emphasizes on mind and intention which shall lead movements, Qi（breath）dropped to Dantian（lower abdomen）, quiet mental state and body relaxation, and the strengthening of the inner part of the body. The organic integration of breathing, inner guiding and the coordination of hands, eyes, body and steps have made Taiji Quan a sport of the unity of inner part and external part. Therefore Taiji Quan is called one of the "Neigong（inner kungfu）Quans".

③ Taiji Quan has adopted ancient Chinese medicine theories of main and the theories of Yin-Yang. According to ancient Chinese medicine theory, Taiji Quan requires "mind and intention to lead breath, guide the Qi（breath）to drive body movements." The inner breath originates from Dantian（lower abdomen）, and drives the strength of the body from the waist. Every style of Taiji Quan uses the theory of Yin-Yang to explain Quan techniques and various changes.

With the development of history, Wushu has changed from battlefield combat to sports fitness, so does Tall Quan. Over 100 years ago, in the "Song of Thirteen Potentials". Taiji masters had pointed out that "What is the ultimate purpose of Taiji? It is to extend longevity." During the long-term circulation, Taiji Quan has developed many schools, among which five schools of Chen-style, Yang-style, Wu-style, Wu-style, and Sun-style are widespread or are provided with relatively obvious characteristics.

Chen-style：There are two styles, an old posture and

种。老架原有七种拳套，历经不断传习和提炼终于形成了近代所传的陈式太极拳第一、二路拳套。新架套路也有两种：种其动作顺序与老架相同，架式与转圈较老架小，去掉了原有的某些难度动作；另一种动作小巧紧凑，练会后逐渐加圈，也称赵堡架。陈式太极拳的运动特点是：显刚隐柔，刚柔相济，动作螺旋、缠绕，手法多变，忽隐忽现，快慢相间；呼吸讲究"丹田内转"；架式宽大低沉，并有发劲、跳跃和震脚动作。

a new posture. The old posture originally had seven sorts of forms. During the continuous teaching, learning, and extraction, they formed the first routine and the second routine of modern Chen-style Taiji Quan. There are two forms of the new posture. One has the same movement sequence as the old posture, but postures and circles are smaller than those of the old posture and some original difficult movements are removed; the other one having small and compact movements and circles can be added during the practice, which is also called Zhaobao Posture. The characteristics of Chen-style Taiji Quan: showing hardness and implying softness, coupling hardness with softness, coiling and twisting the movements with changeable, disappearing, and fast-slow techniques; the breath pays attention to "internal rotation on Dantian"; the postures are involved wide and lowering, power, jumping, and foot stamping.

杨式：创始人为河北永年人杨露禅（1800—1873年），其幼时在河南温县陈家沟陈姓家做僮，从师于陈长兴，壮年返故里，后到北京传习拳艺。经其孙杨澄甫（1883—1936年）的不断修改，遂定型为大架子，成为目前流行最广的杨式太极拳。其特点是：舒展简洁，动作和顺，速度均匀，绵绵不断，整个架式结构严谨，中正圆满，轻灵沉着，浑厚庄重，能自然地表现出气派大、形象美的独特风格。

Yang-style: Yang Luchan (1800—1873), from Yongnian, Hebei, was a houseboy in a Chen family in Wen County, Henan. He learned from Chen Changxing, and went back to his hometown when grew up, then went to Beijng to learn the fist style. Through continuous amendment of his grandson Yang Dengfu (1883—1936), Yang-style had been finally formed into the most popular Yang-style Taiji Quan with a major frame. The characteristics are these: while practicing, the exerciser carries him with poise and confidence and play at medium speed, and its movements are carefully conceived and practically arranged, so as to naturally express the unique style of imposing manner and beauty.

吴式：满族人吴全佑，清末河北大兴人，初拜杨露禅学太极拳大架子，后又拜杨露禅次子杨班侯学小架子，小架子以善柔化而著名。其子吴鉴泉（1870—1942年）在继承父传杨式小架太极拳的基础上对其不断修改，使拳式连绵不断，不纵不跳，使之适应性更广。后人就称之为吴式小架子，即目前流传的吴式太极拳。其特点是：以柔化

Wu-style: Wu Quanyou, Man Minority, from Daxing, Hebei, in the late Qing Dynasty. He had learned major frame of Taiji Quan from Yang Luchan and learned small frame from Yang Luchan's second son Yang Banhou, which was famous for softness. On the basis of Yang-style Taiji Quan with small frame, his son Wu Jianquan (1870—1942) revised Yang-style Taiji Quan into continuous movement without jump, which had relatively wide application. The descendants called the Wu-style small frame that it is the pop-

著称，动作轻松自然，连绵不断，拳式小巧灵活，紧凑中又具舒展，不显拘谨。

武式：创始人为清末河北永年人武禹襄（1812—1880 年），初从师杨露禅，学陈式老架太极拳，得其大概，为求得深造，后又跟陈青萍学陈式新架，经多年演练，自成一家。其特点是：姿势紧凑，动作舒展，步法严格，虚实分明，胸部腹部在进退旋转中始终保持中心，出手不过足尖，左右手各管半个身体。

孙式：清末河北顺平县（原完县）人孙禄堂，精通形意、八卦，民国初向郝为真学太极拳，博采各家之长，融会贯通，独创孙式太极拳。其特点是：进退相随，动作舒展圆活、敏捷自然，转变方向时多以开合相接，故又称"开合活步太极拳"。

新中国成立后，太极拳运动得到蓬勃发展，从 20 世纪 50 年代开始，原国家体委组织专家陆续编写出版了 24 式、48 式、88 式太极拳，又将传统的陈、杨、吴、武、孙式太极拳整理出版。太极拳在国外也得到了广泛的传播，受到各国人民的喜爱。1989 年中国武术研究院编写了适应竞赛的陈、杨、吴、孙式太极拳和综合太极拳的套路，为太极拳进一步向世界推广，迈出了可喜的一步。

太极拳的主要方法有：棚、捋、

ular Wu-style Taiji Quan at present. The characteristics：soft, relax, natural, continuous and flexible. The posture changes from stretching to contracting naturally.

Wu-style：Wu Yuxiang（1812—1880）, from Yongnian, Hebei, in the late Qing Dynasty, He had learned general Chen-style old posture from Yang Luchan for its summary, and then Chen-style New Posture from Chen Qing-ping for advance studies and formed his own style after years of exercises. The characteries：tight postures, extending movements, strict steps, clear in emptiness and solidness. chest or abdomen-centered when advancing, retreating, and rotating, hands within toes, and each hand is in charge of the half body.

Sun-style：Sun Lutang, from Shunping County (used to be called Wan County), Hebei, in the late Qing Dynasty, was proficient in Xingyi Quan and Bagua, who had learned Taiji Quan from Hao Weizhen at the beginning of the Republic of China. He had collected the advantages from all schools and digested to originally create Sun-style Taiji Quan. The characteristics：linked forwards and back ward stepping, extending, swift and natural movements, and direction changes with opening and closing movements. It is also called the "opening and closing flexible step Taiji Quan.

After the establishment of the People's Republic of China, the activity of Taiji Quan has been exploded. Since the 1950s, the State Physical Culture and Sports Commission has organized experts to successfully compile and publish books about 24-style, 88-style, and 48-style Taiji Quan and traditional Chen-style, Yang-style, Wu-style, Wu-style and Sun-style Taiji Quan. Taiji Quan has also been circulated in foreign countries and welcomed by people of different countries. In 1989, the China Wushu Research Institute compiled Chen-style, Yang-style, Wu-style and Sun-style Taiji Quan and forms of comprehensive Taiji Quan, which took a joyful step for further promoting Taiji Quan to the world.

The main methods of Taiji Quan are：the hand tech-

挤、按、采、捌、肘、靠、分、云、推、搂等手法，栽、搬、拦、撇、打等拳法，蹬、分、拍、摆莲等腿法。其运动特点是：心静体松、呼吸自然、轻灵沉着、圆活连贯、上下相随、虚实分明，柔中寓刚、以意导动。

niques of warding-off, rolling-back, pressing, pushing-down, pulling-down, splitting, elbow, leaning, spreading, waving hands like a cloud, pushing, and grabbing; the fist techniques of plunging, deflecting, cutting, sweeping, and striking; as well as the leg techniques of stepping, spreading, clapping, and swing. The characteristics of movements are: quiet heart, relax body, natural breath brisk, continuous, clear between emptiness and solidness, hardness and softness. that can lead to the movements.

第二节 武德与武礼

Section 2　Martial Moralities and Manners

一、武德含义

1. The meaning of martial moralities

中国素有礼仪之邦的美称，历来重礼仪、重伦理。武术是以拳脚和器械进行对抗的运动，稍一疏忽就会伤人。所以，古时训练兵勇或教授徒弟，都特别讲究武德，点到为止，不能伤人。因此，历代武术家将"德"作为武术之根本，各类武术门派的拳谱、家法，开宗明义都要阐明武德，并规定必须遵守的道德规范。到现代，武术界将武德规范概括为"尚武崇德，修身养性"。

China has long been known as a nation of etiquette. It has always attached great importance to etiquette and ethics. Martial arts is an exercise in which fists, feet, and equipment fight against each other, and a slight negligence may hurt people. Therefore, in ancient times, people paid particular attention to martial moralities when training soldiers or apprentices. Do not go further than necessary to avoid hurting people. Therefore, the martial arts experts of all ages regard "ethics" as the foundation of martial arts. The spectrum and family rules of various martial arts schools must clearly explain martial moralities and stipulate the moral standards that must be followed. In modern times, the martial arts circle has summarized the martial arts norms as "Value martial moralities and behave properly to improve your character".

太极拳的学拳须知：

Instructions for Taiji Quan:

① 学太极拳不可不敬，不敬则外慢师友，内慢身体，心不敛束，何能学艺。

① Don't be disrespectful when learning Taiji Quan. Treating your teacher without respect may also hurt your body. You can never learn art if your heart is not constricted.

② 学太极拳不可狂，狂则生是非。

② Don't be wildly arrogant when learning Taiji Quan, if not, you may stir up trouble.

③ 学太极拳不可满，满则招损。

③ Never be self-satisfied when learning Taiji Quan, or you will stand to lose.

④ 学太极拳,每个动作都应当细心揣摩。

⑤ 学太极拳先学读书,书理明白,学拳自然容易。

二、抱拳礼

抱拳礼是武术活动中的基本礼节。

(1) 行礼方法

并步站立,左手四指并拢伸直成掌,拇指屈拢;右手成拳,左掌心掩贴右拳面,左指尖与下颌平齐。右拳眼斜对胸窝,置于胸前屈臂成圆,肘尖略下垂,拳掌与胸相距20~30厘米。头正,身直,目视受礼者,面容举止自然大方。

(2) 具体含义

左掌表示德、智、体、美"四育"齐备,象征高尚情操,大拇指内屈指表示不自大,不骄傲,不以"老大"自居。右拳表示勇猛习武。左掌掩右拳相抱,表示"勇不滋乱""止戈为武",有以此来约束、节制勇武的意思。

左掌右拳拢屈,两臂屈圆,表示五湖四海皆兄弟,天下武林是一家,谦虚团结,以武会友。

左掌为文,右拳为武,文武兼学,虚心、渴望求知,恭候师友、前辈指教。

④ Every moment should be carefully considered.

⑤ You should learn to read books before learning Taiji Quan. If you can understand them, learning Taiji Quan will be quite easy.

2. Fist-palm salute

Fist-palm salute is the basic etiquette in martial arts activities.

(1) Salute method

Stand side by side, stretch your left fingers together to straighten your palms, and bend your thumbs; your right hand make a fist, cover your right fist with your left palm, and your left fingertip flush with your chin. Your right fist eye is oblique to the chest, and should be placed in front of the chest to bend the arms round, the elbow tip is slightly drooping, and the fist palm should keep 20-30 cm away from the chest. Keep your head and your body straight, your eyes towards the recipient and your face and behavior natural.

(2) Specific meaning

The left palm indicates that the "four educations" of morality, intelligence, physique and beauty are in place, symbolizing the noble sentiment. Flexion of thumb indicates no arrogance, no pride and no self-promotion. The right fist indicates brave martial arts. The left palm covers the right fist and embraces each other, which means "brave is not disturbing" and "stop the war for martial arts" in order to restrain and restrain the bravery.

The left palm and the right fist are bent, and the arms are rounded, indicating that all the lakes and brothers are brothers. The martial art circle is a family in which you should be humble and united to make friends with same interest in it.

The left palm stands for culture while the right fist for martial arts, you should be eager to learn both of them humbly, always humbly waiting for advice from teachers and seniors.

第五章　太极拳技术分析及训练方法
Chapter 5　Technical Analysis on and Training Methods of Taiji Quan

本章要点：本章主要讲述太极拳的运动特点、技术分析、技术训练方法。

Key points: The chapter mainly introduces the sports features of, technical analysis on and training methods of Taiji Quan.

第一节　太极拳的运动风格

Section 1　Sports Style of Taiji Quan

（1）体松心静

体松心静是太极拳的运动特点之一。"体松"是指在练拳时，身体肌肉处于一种放松状态，使身体自然舒展，不得用僵力。"心静"是指练拳时要排除一切杂念，注意力要集中。

（1）*Relax body and peaceful heart*

The "relax body and peaceful heart" is one of the movement characteristics of Taiji Quan. The "relax body" means that the body muscles are in relax status during the practice and the body is naturally stretched without the rigid force. The "peaceful heart" means that you should remove all the distracting thoughts and pay attention.

（2）缓慢柔和

缓慢柔和也是太极拳的运动特点。一套简化太极拳，二十四个动作，按正常速度需要在5～6分钟之间完成，缓慢还需要连贯，即动作连绵不断，而柔的前提是要放松，在此基础上，两臂的姿势及运动路线都要保持弧形。

（2）*Slow and gentle strength*

The slow and gentle strength is also the characteristic of Taiji Quan. A set of simplified Taiji Quan has 24 movements, which shall be finished in about 5 to 6 minutes at normal speed. It requires slow but continuous strength, namely the successive movements with the premise of the softness of relaxing. On that basis, the postures and moving lines of two arms shall be maintained to keep in a curve.

（3）动作、呼吸和意念相配合

初学时要保持自然呼吸，练习到一定程度时，须将呼吸、意念相配合。太极拳的呼吸一般都是与动作相配合的，即起吸、落呼、开吸、合呼，如起势、收势动作，两臂向上抬起时吸气，下落

（3）*Coordination of movement, breath, and mind*

A new learner should keep natural breath at the beginning of learning Taiji Quan. After some practice, the coordination of breath and mind is required. The breath of Taiji Quan shall generally be coordinated with movements: inhale when rising, exhale when

时呼气；两手张开时吸气，合时呼气。另一种呼吸方式为：凡是一个动作完成时为呼气，过渡动作时为吸气。还可以理解为，向外进攻的动作为呼气，进攻前的动作为吸气。无论哪一种呼吸方式都应力求自然。动作与意念的配合，就是练拳时要排除一切杂念把注意力集中到动作上。以意识引导动作，做到"意领身随"。

falling, inhale when opening, and exhale when closing. For example, for the movements of rising and closing, you shall inhale when rising the arms, and exhale when falling the aims. In addition, you shall inhale when opening hands, and exhale when closing hands. Another way of breath is that: exhale when completing a movement and inhale when changing movement, or exhale when attacking and inhale before attacking. No matter which way of breath it should be natural. The coordination of movements and mind means that you must remove all the distracting thoughts when practicing, and pay attention to the movements. The consciousness should lead the movements, then make the "entire body follow the mind".

第二节　太极拳的技术分析

Section 2　Technical Analysis of Taiji Quan

（1）虚灵顶劲

（1）Empty butting force

虚灵顶劲即"顶头悬"。练拳时讲究头部的头正、顶平、项直、颏收，要求头顶的百会穴处要向上轻轻顶起，同时又须保持头顶的平正。要使头正、顶平，就必须使颈项竖直、下颏里收。顶劲不可过分用力，要有自然虚之意，做到虚灵顶劲，精神才提得起来，动作才能沉稳、扎实。

The empty butting force namely "pull the head up straight with one's intention. as if the hair were hanging up to the ceiling". The head shall be upright, the top of the head shall be flat, the nape shall be straight, and the mandible shall be withdrawn. The butting force cannot be too strong, but shall be natural and empty. Only keeping mind empty that the spirit can be raised and movements can be stable and strong.

（2）气沉丹田

（2）Gathering qi into dantian

气沉丹田，是身法端正，宽胸实腹，"意注丹田"，意识引导呼吸，将气徐徐送到腹部脐下。太极拳在运动时，一般都是采用腹式呼吸，同时"意注丹田"，这样能达到太极拳"身动、心静、气敛、神舒"的境地。用腹式呼吸来加深气息，应自然、匀细、徐徐吞吐，呼吸要与动作自然配合，不能用强制的方法。要求一呼一吸与整套动作结合得非常密切，应根据动作的开合、屈伸、起落、进退、虚实等变化，自然地去配合。一般地说，呼吸总是与胸廓的张缩、肩胛的活动自然结合着。在一个动

Requires the upright body techniques, the wide chest, and the solid abdomen. "Filling mind into Dantian", the consciousness shall lead the breath, gently send Qi to be under the navel of the abdomen. During the movement, Taiji Quan generally adopts the abdomen breath, and "fills mind into Dantian", so as to achieve the circumstances of "moving body, peaceful heart, constricting breath, and extending spirit". Abdomen-style breathing is adopted to deepen and prolong the breath which shall be natural, equable, slow and coordinated with the movements. Forcibleness shall be prevented and the whole set of movements, including opening, closing, bending, stretching. Rising, falling, forwarding, re-

作里，往往就伴随着一呼一吸，而不是一个动作固定为一吸或是一呼。这种与动作自然配合的方法运用得当，可以使动作更加协调、圆活、轻灵、沉稳。

treating, feinted moving, intended moving, etc., it shall be in good and natural coordination with breathing. Generally speaking, the breathing is always naturally in coordination with the pumping of the chest and the movement of the blade bones. The completion of a movement is usually accompanied by a round of breathing instead of inhaling or exhaling only. Such a good command and application of this breathing method as in natural coordination with movements that are necessary to make the movement coordinative. flexible, agile, light and steady.

(3) 含胸拔背

含胸是胸廓略向内涵虚，使胸部有舒宽的感觉。这样有利于做好腹式呼吸，能在肩锁关节放松、两肩微含、两肋微敛的姿势下，通过动作使胸腔上下径放长，横膈有下降舒展的机会。它既能使重心下降，又使肺脏、横膈活动加强。拔背与含胸是相互联系的，要含胸就势必拔背。拔背是在胸略向内虚时背部肌肉向下松沉，两肩中间颈下第三脊骨鼓起上提并略向后上方拉起，不能单纯地往后拉。这样背部肌肉就会有一定的张、弹力，皮肤有绷紧的感觉。含胸拔背，胸背肌肉须松沉，不能故意做作。

(3) Relaxing the chest and drawing the back

The chest relaxing is that the chest is slightly and internally relaxed, so as to make the chest have a comfortable feeling, thus being favor of making the abdomen breath. When the shoulder is relaxed and the rib is drawn. The thoracic cavity will be relaxed and extended. It can not only drop the center of gravity and can strengthen the lungs and the diaphragm. The back drawing and chest relaxing are mutually connected. The back drawing means that when relaxing the chest, the muscles on the back should be relaxed and dropped down. The third vertebra shall rise and draw upwards and backwards, which can't simply pull backwards. Thus stretching the back muscles for the tension and elasticity, so that the skin will have the tightening feeling. The muscles of the chest and the back should be relaxed and natural without the deliberate pretense.

(4) 松腰敛臀

太极拳要求合胸、沉气，因此在含胸时就必须松腰。松腰不仅帮助沉气和下肢的稳固，更主要的是它对动作的进退旋转、用躯干带动四肢的活动及动作的完整性，起着主导作用。敛臀则是在含胸拔背和松腰的基础上使臀部稍作内收。敛臀时，可尽量放松臀、腰部肌肉，使臀肌向外下方舒展，然后轻轻向前、向里收敛，像用臀把小腹托起来似的。

(4) Relaxing the waist and drawing the butt

Taiji Quan requires chest closing and breath dropping. The waist relaxing can not only help to drop the breath and fixing the lower limbs, and it also plays a leading role in the forwards and backwards stepping and rotation, movements of limbs, as well as the completion of movements. The butt drawing means to draw in the butt after relaxing chest, drawing back and relaxing waist. When drawing the butt, you shall try to relax muscles of the butt and waist, extend the muscles, and then draw in it like the butt is supporting the abdomen.

（5）圆裆松胯

裆即会阴部位。头顶百会穴的"虚灵顶劲"要与会阴穴上下相应，这是保持身法端正、气贯上下的锻炼方法。裆要圆，又要实。胯撑开，两膝微向里扣，裆自圆。会阴处虚上提，裆自会实；加上腰的松沉、臀的收敛，自然产生裆劲。太极拳讲究"迈步如猫行"，要求步法轻灵稳健，两腿弯曲轮换支持身体进行活动。因此髋部关节须放松，膝关节须灵活，才能保证上体旋转自如，踢腿、换步灵便。

（6）沉肩坠肘

太极拳在松肩的前提下要求沉肩坠肘，两臂由于肩、肘的下坠会有一种沉重的内劲，这就是上肢内在的遒劲。两肩除沉之外，还要有些微向前合抱的意思，这能使胸部完全涵虚，使脊背团成圆形。两肘下坠之外，也要有一些微向里的裹劲。这样的沉肩坠肘，才能使劲力贯串到上肢手臂。

（7）舒指坐腕

舒指是掌指自然伸展，坐腕是腕关节向手背、虎口的一侧自然屈起。掌的动作是整体动作的一部分，许多掌法都是与全身动作连成一气的，因此舒指坐腕，实际是将周身劲力通过"其根在脚，发于腿，主宰于腰，形于手指"完整的。

（8）尾闾中正

尾闾中正是关系身躯、动作姿势"中正安舒""支撑八面"的准星。因之太极拳运动时极重视尾闾中正，不论是直的或是斜的动作姿势，都必须保持尾闾与脊椎成直线，处于中正状态。更重

(5) Drawing in the crotch in a circle and relaxing the hipbone

The crotch is the perineum part, which is corresponding to the "empty butting force" on the head up and down. It is the exercising method of maintaining the straight body forms straight with a smooth breath. The hipbones shall be open, the two knees shall be slight point inwards, and the crotch shall be in a circle. Rise the crotch, and it shall be solid. Relax the waist draws in the butt and it shall bring force to the crotch. Taiji Quan pays attention to "making steps like a cat" which requires the light, flexible and stable step techniques. Two legs shall be bent and support the body in turns. The hip shall be relaxed and knees shall be flexible so as to guarantee the free rotation of the upper body in flexible kicking and changing steps.

(6) Dropping the shoulders and dropping the elbows

After relaxing the shoulders, shoulders and elbows shall be dropped The dropping of shoulders and elbows will bring a heavy inner force, which is the inner force of upper limbs. Except for dropping, the shoulders shall also be closing forwards which make the chest empty and the back roll in a circle. Besides dropping, the elbows shall also be inward so that the force can go up to the arms when dropping the shoulders.

(7) Extending fingers and sitting wrists

Extending fingers means that fingers are extended naturally. Sitting wrists means that the wrists bend towards the back of hands and Hukou naturally. The movements of palms are the part of movements of the body, and many palm techniques are connected with movements of the body. Extending fingers and sitting wrists drive the force from feet and legs to the fingers and to complete it.

(8) Keeping the coccygeal vertebrae straight

It keeps the posture of the body straight, relaxing and supporting. Taiji Quan emphasizes on it. The coccygeal vertebrae shall always be straight in any other movement posture. Moreover, keeping coccygeal vertebrae straight affects the stableness of the lower

要的是，尾闾中正还影响着下盘的稳固。所以尾闾中正同样是和以上七点连贯统一的。能够统一地做到这八点，就可以使躯干、上肢、下肢的内在劲力达到完整如一。

（9）内宜鼓荡，外示安逸

鼓荡是对内在精神所提的要求，鼓荡是精神振奋的意思。内宜鼓荡是说内在的精神要振奋，然而这种振奋是沉着的，"神宜内敛"的，并不流于形色，表现是安逸的。

（10）运动如抽丝，迈步如猫行

太极拳运动要像抽丝那样既缓又匀、又稳又静，迈步又要像猫那样轻起轻落，提步、落步都要有轻灵的感觉。静是太极拳特点之一，练太极拳首要的条件就是要做到心里安静，排除杂念，使精神完全集中到运动上来。心静，才能"用意不用力"，使运动像抽丝那样安静。太极拳讲究"用意识引导动作"，是一种"会意"的运动。"缓以会意"，只有徐缓地活动才能会意，因此它要求运动像抽丝那样徐缓不躁。太极拳又讲究速度均匀，要求保持适当的等速运动，又须像抽丝那样均匀地抽拉。其步法必须相应地像猫迈步那样轻灵。

第三节 太极拳的训练方法

太极拳运动在训练中要求内外结合和动静结合。内外结合，就是外求形体动作的准确与完整，内求意识指导动作和呼吸的配合，进而达到手眼身法步和心志意气的内外统一。动静结合，就是静止性的定势练习和活动性的动作练习相结合，如各种站桩、动作定势练习与步型转换动作组合相结合等。尤其是进行完整的技术动作训练时，一定要"动中有静，静中有动"，这样才能有效地提高太极拳所需要的专项素质和形成正

limbs. If one can fulfill the above-mentioned seven instructions integrally with this one, the force of the body, upper limbs, lower limbs will be perfectly integrated.

(9) Exciting inside, and calm outside

The spirit shall be exciting and energetic. But the excitement shall be inside and the outside shall be calm and relax.

(10) Movements like drawing silk, stepping like cat-walk

The movements of Taiji Quan shall be slow, smooth, stable, and quiet as if drawing silk and stepping shall be light as a cat. Taiji Quan shall be quiet, and quietness is the characteristic of Taiji. The prime condition of Taiji Quan is that the mind shall be quiet and pure without any distraction and shall focus on movements. Only the heart is peaceful, the movements can be quiet like drawing silk and "using mind not force". Taiji Quan pays attention to using the "consciousness to lead movements." It is a "will" sport. "Being slow to express the will", the will can be expressed only being slow. Taiji Quan also requires the speed to be even and smooth like drawing silk and stepping like cat-walk.

Section 3 Training Methods of Taiji Quan

Taiji Quan sports in the training requires the combination of internal and external and dynamic and static combination. The combination of inside and outside means the accuracy and integrity of the movement of the external body and the cooperation of the action and breath guided by the inner consciousness so as to achieve the unity of the hand-eye-body step and the spirit of mind and spirit inside and outside. The combination of dynamic and static is the combination of static fixed practice and active exercise, such as the combination of various stations and piles, the combination of action fixing exercise and the combination

确的动力定型，从而提高套路运动的技术水平。内外结合、动静结合的要求要贯彻训练的全过程。

　　太极拳的训练内容包括基本功、基本动作和套路技术训练，其目的是增进练习者健康，促进练习者身心的发展，使练习者掌握太极拳需要的各种活动技能，并在此基础上不断提高太极拳技术水平。

一、基本功训练

　　太极拳基本功是掌握和提高太极拳技术的基础训练，是端正身体基本姿势、提高身心专项素质、壮内健外的根本训练环节。借鉴前人经验，根据我们长期教学训练实践，选定了"太极桩""开合桩""升降桩""虚步桩"作为太极拳的"基本功"练习。

（1）太极桩

　　两脚平行分开与肩同宽，两膝微屈，重心落于两腿之间。两臂微屈，举于胸前，手指微屈，自然展开，指尖相对（相距约20厘米），掌心向里做抱球状，目视两手之间。上体正直，头正悬顶，下颏微收，沉肩垂肘，松腰敛臀，精神集中，意守丹田，呼吸自然，初练每次5分钟，久练逐渐增加。姿势高低可根据体质和腿部力量掌握，通过练习使下部力量增加，重心沉稳，周身内劲

of step-by-step transformation movement, and so on. Especially when carrying on the complete technical movement training, must "move in the movement, static in the movement", only in this way can we effectively improve the special quality required by Taiji Quan and form the correct dynamic stereotyping, so as to improve the routine operation. The technical level of movement. The combination of internal and external, dynamic and static needs to carry out the whole process of training.

The training contents of Taiji Quan include basic skills, basic movements and routine techniques, the purpose of which is to improve the health of the practitioner, to promote the physical and mental development of the practitioner, and to master the various activities and skills required by Taiji Quan. And on this basis, constantly improve the technical level of Taiji Quan.

1. Basic training

The basic skill of Taiji Quan is the basic training to master and improve the Taiji Quan technique, it is the basic training link to correct the basic posture of the body, to improve the special quality of body and mind, and to strengthen the internal and external health. Based on the experience of predecessors and our long-term teaching practice, "Taiji pile", "opening and closing pile", "lifting and closing pile", "up-and-down pile", "foot-stepping pile" are selected as the "basic skills" of Taiji Quan.

（1） *Taiji pile*

Feet are parallel to the shoulders' width, knees slightly flexed, the center of gravity lay between the legs. Arms are slightly flexed, raised in front of the chest, fingers flexed naturally, the tip of the finger opposite (about 20 cm apart), the centre of the palms to hug a ball, visual between the two hands. Upper body integrity, head hanging top, chin micro-retract, shoulder down elbow, loose waist and buttocks, concentration, intent to guard Dantian, breathing naturally, 5 minutes of initial training, long training gradually increased. Posture can be mastered

饱满，丹田之气充实。

according to physique and leg strength, through practice to increase the lower strength, center of gravity steady, full of internal strength, Dantian full of gas.

(2) 开合桩

在太极桩姿势的基础上，两手臂做稍向外开和稍向内收合的练习。"开"时为"吸气"（小腹鼓起），"合"时为"呼气"（小腹内收）。初练时，呼吸应力求自然通畅，不要勉强，练久之后，可加大呼吸深度，扩大充气量，如吸到极点不能再吸时，改为呼气；同样呼到极点不能再呼时，改为吸气。这样，每次可练3～5分钟，练久可逐渐增加。

(2) *Open and close pile*

On the basis of Taiji pile posture, the arms do a little outward and slightly inward. When "open", "inhale" (lower abdomen bulging), "close" "exhale" (lower abdomenl receptacle). Initial training, breathing should strive for natural patency, do not reluctantly, after a long time, can increase breathing depth, expand the volume of air. If you can't breathe at the pole, exhale; if you can't breathe again at the pole, breathe in. In this way, you can practice 3 minutes to 5 minutes at a time, the training time can gradually increase.

(3) 升降桩

身体自然正直，两脚开立，头正悬顶，下颌微收，肩臂松垂，两手轻贴大腿外侧，眼向前平视。这时身体放松，心静，排除杂念，精神集中，呼吸自然。

(3) *Lifting pile*

Natural integrity, feet open, head hanging, chin micro-retract, shoulders and arms loose, both hands gently to the outside of the thigh, eyes forward. At this time the body relaxes, the mind is quiet, removes the miscellaneous thought, the spirit is concentrated, breathes naturally.

(4) 虚步桩

立正，重心移至右腿并屈膝，左脚向左前方迈进半步，脚跟着地，脚尖翘起，左膝微屈。同时两掌向左前上方举起，左掌指同鼻高，右掌在左肘内下方，两掌指微屈，自然分开，掌心斜向对，指尖均朝上方，眼看左掌方向，如同左琵琶势。

(4) *Virtual step pile*

Standing attention, the center of gravity moved to the right leg and bent knee, left foot forward half a step to the left, heel to the ground, the tip of the foot raised, the left knee slightly flexed. At the same time, both palms are raised to the left and up, the left palm is high with nose, the right palm is in the lower part of the left elbow, the two palm fingers are slightly flexed, naturally separated, the center of the palm is tilted toward each other, the tips of the fingers are all facing upward, and the left metacarpal looks like left Biwako.

二、基本动作训练

基本动作就是代表太极拳风格、特点，具有普遍性、规律性的典型动作，是该拳整个套路技术的核心动作。在教学训练的实践中，我们选定"倒卷肱""云手""野马分鬃""金鸡独立""搂膝

2. Basic motion training

The basic movements represent the style, characteristics, universality and regularity of Taiji Quan, which is the core of the whole routine technique of Taiji Quan. In the practice of teaching and training, we selected such typical movements as "turning back

拗步""捋挤势""蹬脚"和"揽雀尾"等典型动作作为太极拳的基本动作，进行反复练习，以外引内，以内导外，内外结合，使基本功训练获得的素质和体能通过太极拳技法理论的指导得到提高，提高基本动作质量，使动作规范化。通过基本动作的训练，使练习者掌握太极拳基本技术规律，从而提高套路技术水平。

进行基本动作训练时，每个动作先原地左右重复练习，再行进间左右重复练习。

三、套路技术训练

太极拳技术水平的高低，是通过套路演练表现的。太极拳套路主要由基本动作组合而成。基本动作训练中所获得的技术水平，往往直接影响着套路的成绩。但是套路又不等于单纯的单个动作的总和。套路要求动作与动作之间有贯穿一气的联系，要绵绵不断，势势相承。为此，在强调单个动作训练的同时还必须强调动作的反复训练。所谓"拳打千遍，身法自然"就是这个道理。

the humerus", "Yunshou", "Mustang split bristle", "Golden Chicken Independence", "kneading the knees", "stroking the legs", "pedaling the foot" and "taking the tail of the bird" as the basic movements of Taiji Quan. In order to improve the quality and normalize the basic movement, the quality and physical ability obtained by the training of basic skills can be obtained through the guidance of the theory of Taiji Quan technique, and the quality of basic movements can be improved and standardized by repeated exercises, with the introduction of the internal and external guidance and the combination of internal and external guidance. Through the training of basic movements, the practitioner can master Taiji Quan basic technical rules, so as to improve the technical level of routine.

During the basic movement training, each movement should be repeated in situ and left and right first, and then left and right between marches.

3. Routine technique training

The technical level of Taiji Quan is expressed through routine exercises. Taiji Quan routines are mainly composed of basic actions. The skill level obtained in basic movement training often directly affects the performance of the routine. But the routine is not equal to the sum of simple individual actions. Routine requires that there is a running-through relationship between the movement and the movement, to be continuous, the momentum is inherited. To this end, it is necessary to emphasize the repeated training of movements while emphasizing the training of individual movements. The so-called "punches a thousand times, the natural body method" is this truth.

第六章　24式太极拳动作图解
Chapter 6　The Movement Illustration of Twenty-four Style Taiji Quan

本章要点：本章通过183幅动作图片和9段高清视频（视频全部配有中英文字幕），详细讲述了太极拳的基本功和24式太极拳的练习方法。

Key points：With 183 motion diagrams and 10 HD videos accompanied with Chinese and English subtitles, the chapter introduces the basic techniques of and exercise methods for Twenty-four Style Taiji Quan in detail.

第一节　基本功

一、手型

（1）掌

虚掌：五指自然舒松，掌心内凹涵空，意念吸引力量（图3-1）。

实掌：五指自然伸展，掌心微向前撑，意念按压力量（图6-1）。

Section 1　Basic Techniques

1. Hands

（1）*Palm*

Empty Palm：Five fingers relax naturally. Hold the center of the palm inset. Use the mind to draw power（Fig 3-1）.

Solid Palm：Five fingers open naturally with the centre of the palm forward slightly. Use the mind to press（Fig. 6-1）.

图 6-1　(Fig. 6-1)

图 6-2　(Fig. 6-2)

图 6-3　(Fig. 6-3)

(2) 拳

四指内卷，拇指压在食指、中指的中节，握拳舒松而内含力量（图6-2）。

(3) 勾

屈腕，五指第一指节捏拢（图6-3）。

二、步型

(1) 弓步

两腿前后分开约一腿长，横向距离约一脚长；前脚脚尖朝正前，前腿膝关节弯曲，呈屈蹲姿势，膝盖不过脚尖；后腿膝关节自然伸直，全脚掌着地，脚尖外开45°（图6-4、图6-5）。

(2) *Fist*

Bend four fingers with your thumb pressing the middle of the index finger and middle finger, and make a relaxed fist with strength inside (Fig. 6-2).

(3) *Hook*

Bend your wrist and hold the first knuckles of five fingers together (Fig. 6-3).

2. Stance

(1) *Bow stance*

Put one foot forward with tiptoes facing forward, keeping a leg distance lengthwise and a foot distance crosswise with the other, front knee bending with thigh slanting to the ground and knee above tiptoes; meanwhile, the other leg is stretching naturally with whole foot on the ground, tiptoes turning outward 45 degrees (Fig. 6-4, Fig. 6-5).

图6-4　(Fig. 6-4)

图6-5　(Fig. 6-5)

(2) 虚步

前脚脚跟着地，勾脚尖，微屈膝；后腿屈膝下蹲，脚尖外开45°，全脚掌着地；身体重心放于后腿（图6-6）。

(2) *Empty stance*

Rest the heel of the front foot on the ground with tiptoes tilting upward and knee slightly bent; bend rear leg with whole foot on the ground and tiptoes turning outward 45 degrees. Bodyweight rests on the rear leg (Fig. 6-6).

图 6-6 （Fig. 6-6）　　　　图 6-7 （Fig. 6-7）

（3）仆步

仆步是一种低步法，也称"单跌岔"，一腿屈膝下蹲，一腿伸直铺地，但不能全坐死，臀部离地约10厘米，使裆内有灵活旋转力，是练习腿部支撑力的一种方法，如"左下势独立"（图 6-7）。

（4）独立步

独立步是一种高步法，恰和仆步对称，一高一低。它是一腿站立支撑身体重心，另一腿屈膝提起，膝高与胯平，脚尖内扣，旋于裆内。站立之腿挺而不直，要稳重自然，如"金鸡独立"（图 6-8）。

（5）左坐盘

左坐盘步是右腿在前，左腿在后，交叉盘腿下坐，如"左右倒卷肱"等。要求右腿支撑重心，左腿虚足，脚尖点地，屈膝下蹲。右坐盘与左坐盘动作要领相同，只是左右相反（图 6-9）。

（3）*Butcher's stance*

A butcher step is a low-step method, also known as a "single drop", one leg bent knee squat, one leg spread straight floor, but not all sit dead, hips about 10 centimeters away from the ground, so that there is flexible rotation in the crotch, is a way to practice leg support, For example, "Push Down and Stand on the Left Foot" and so on（Fig. 6-7）.

（4）*One leg stance*

The independent step is a kind of high-step method, it is symmetrical with the servant step, one is high and one is low. It is one leg standing to support the center of gravity, the other leg bent, lift the knee height to the crotch level, the tip of the foot buckle, rotated in the file. Standing legs upright and not straight, should be stable and natural, such as "golden chicken standing on one foot"（Fig. 6-8）.

（5）*Left disk*

The "left disk" is the right leg in the front, the left leg in the back, cross under the leg, such as "backward steps and swirling arms on both sides" and so on . The right leg is required to support the center of gravity, the left leg is weak, the foot point is pointed, and the knee is bent and squat. The right-hand and left-seated movements are the same, but the opposite is left and right（Fig. 6-9）.

图 6-8　(Fig. 6-8)

图 6-9　(Fig. 6-9)

第二节　动作图解

动作名称

预备式

第一组

一　起势

二　左右野马分鬃

三　白鹤亮翅

第二组

四　左右搂膝拗步

五　手挥琵琶

六　左右倒卷肱

第三组

七　左揽雀尾

八　右揽雀尾

第四组

九　单鞭

十　云手

十一　单鞭

第五组

十二　高探马

十三　右蹬脚

十四　双峰贯耳

十五　转身左蹬脚

第六组

十六　左下势独立

Section 2　Illustration of Movement

Name of Movement

Preparing

Group 1

1　Opening

2　Splitting the Wild Horse's Mane on Both Sides

3　White Crane Spreads It's Wing

Group 2

4　Brush Knee and Twist Step on Both Sides

5　Playing the Pipa

6　Backward Steps and Swirling Arms on Both Sides

Group 3

7　Grasp the Peacock's Tail-Left Style

8　Grasp the Peacock's Tail-Right Style

Group 4

9　Single Whip

10　Wave Hands Like Clouds

11　Single Whip

Group 5

12　High Pat on Horse

13　Kick with the Right Heel

14　Striking Ears with Both Fists

15　Body Turning and Left Heel Kicking

Group 6

16　Push Down and Stand on the Left Foot

| 十七 | 右下势独立 | 17 | Push Down and Stand on the Right Foot |

第七组

Group 7

十八	左右穿梭	18	Working with a Shuttle on Both Sides
十九	海底针	19	Needle to the Bottom of the Sea
二十	闪通臂	20	Flashing the Arm

第八组

Group 8

二一	转身搬拦捶	21	Turn to Deflect Downwards Parry and Punch
二二	如封似闭	22	Apparent Close-up
二三	十字手	23	Crossing Hands
二四	收势	24	Closing

动作图解

预备式

身体自然站立，两脚并拢，脚尖向前，两臂垂于身体两侧，手指微屈，中指轻贴于裤缝，头顶正直，口闭齿叩，舌抵上腭，肩、胯、膝、胸、腹均要自然放松，精神集中，两眼平视，表情自然。

Illustration of Movement

Preparing

Maintain a natural upright position. Place the feet together and toes pointing forward. Arms are beside both sides of the body. Bend the fingers slightly, the middle one on the sewing lines of the pants. Head and neck is upright, the mouth is closed. The tongue is at the roof of the mouth. Shoulders, hips, knees, chest, and abdomen have to be naturally relaxed, mind concentrated. Eyes see straight forward. Keep face express naturally.

■ 第一组

一 起势

① 重心向右腿移动，右腿微屈，左脚跟提起，左脚大脚趾着地，然后左脚提起向左侧分开，由左脚大脚趾先着地，再依次脚掌、脚跟，全脚着地，身体自然直立，两脚开立，与肩同宽，脚尖向前，两臂自然下垂，两手放在大腿外侧，眼向前平看（图6-10）。

要点：头颈正直，下颏微向后收，不要故意挺胸或收腹。精神要集中（起势由立正姿势开始，然后左脚向左分开，成开立步）。

② 两臂慢慢向前平举，两手高与肩平，与肩同宽，手心向下（图6-11、图6-12）。

■ Group 1

1 Opening

① Shift the weight to the right leg and bend the leg slightly. Raise the left heel first and step to the left, with toes touching the ground first, then the forefoot, then the heel. Stand upright with feet shoulder-width apart, toes pointing forward, arms hanging naturally at sides. Look straight ahead (Fig. 6-10).

太极拳　第一组

Points to Remember: Hold head and neck erect with chin drawn slightly inward. Do not protrude chest or draw abdomen in.

② Raise arms slowly forward to the shoulder level with palms down (Fig. 6-11, Fig. 6-12).

图 6-10 （Fig. 6-10）　　图 6-11 （Fig. 6-11）　　图 6-12 （Fig. 6-12）

③ 上体保持正直，两腿屈膝下蹲；同时两掌轻轻下按，两肘下垂与两膝相对；眼睛平视前方（图 6-13）。

要点：两肩下沉，两肘松垂，手指自然微屈。屈膝松腰，臀部不可凸出，身体重心落于两腿中间。两臂下落和身体下蹲的动作要协调一致。

二　左右野马分鬃

① 上体微向右转，身体重心移至右腿上；同时右臂收在胸前平屈，手心向下，左手经体前向右下画弧放在右手下，手心向上，两手心相对成抱球状；左脚随即收到右脚内侧，脚尖点地；眼看右手（图 6-14、图 6-15）。

② 上体微向左转，左脚向左前方迈出，右脚跟后蹬，右腿自然伸直，成左弓步；同时上体继续向左转，左右手随转体慢慢分别向左上右下分开，左

③ Bend knees as you press palms down gently with elbows dropping towards knees. Look straight ahead (Fig. 6-13)

Points to Remember：Keep torso erect and hold shoulders and elbows down. Fingers are slightly curved. The body weight is equally distributed between legs while bending knees, keep waist relaxed and buttocks slightly pulled in. The lowering of arms should be coordinated with the bending of knees.

2　Splitting the wild horses mane on both side

① With body turning slightly to the right and weight shifted onto the right leg, raise the right hand until the forearm lies horizontally in front of the right part of the chest, while the left hand moves in a downward curve until it comes under the right hand, palms facing each other as if holding a ball (henceforth referred to as "hold-ball gesture"). Move the left foot to the side of the right foot, toes on the floor. Look at the right hand (Fig. 6-14, Fig. 6-15).

② Turn the body to the left as the left foot takes a step towards 11-12 o'clock. Bending knee and shifting weight onto the left leg, while the right leg straightens with the whole foot on the floor for a left "bow

手高与眼平（手心斜向上），肘微屈；右手落在右胯旁，肘也微屈，手心向下，指尖向前；眼看左手（图6-16至图6-18）。

stance". As you turn the body, raise the left hand to eye level with the palm facing obliquely up and elbow slightly bent, and lower the right hand to the side of the right hip with the palm facing down and fingers pointing forward. Look at the left hand (Fig. 6-16 to Fig. 6-18).

图 6-13　(Fig. 6-13)　　图 6-14　(Fig. 6-14)　　图 6-15　(Fig. 6-15)

图 6-16　(Fig. 6-16)　　图 6-17　(Fig. 6-17)　　图 6-18　(Fig. 6-18)

③ 上体慢慢后坐，身体重心移至右腿，左脚尖翘起，微向外撇（大约45°～60°），随后脚掌慢慢踏实，左腿慢慢前弓，身体左转，身体重心再移至左腿；同时左手翻转向下，左臂收在胸前平屈，右手向左上划弧放在左手下，两手心相对成抱球状；右脚随即收到左脚内侧，脚尖点地；眼看左手（图6-19至图6-21）。

③ "Sit back" slowly and body backward as if ready to take a seat, and shift weight onto the right leg. Raising toes of the left foot. Slightly and turning them outward before placing the whole foot on the floor. Then bend the left leg and turn the body to the left, shifting weight onto the left leg and making a hold-ball gesture in front of the left part of the chest with the left hand on top. Then move the right foot to the side of the left foot with toes on the floor. Look at the left hand (Fig. 6-19 to Fig. 6-21).

图6-19 (Fig. 6-19)

图6-20 (Fig. 6-20)

图6-21 (Fig. 6-21)

④ 右腿向右前方迈出，左腿自然伸直，成右弓步；同时上体右转，左右手随转体分别慢慢向左下右上分开，右手高与眼平（手心斜向上），肘微屈；左手落在左胯旁，肘也微屈，手心向下，指尖向前；眼看右手（图6-22、图6-23）。

④ Take a right bow stance by moving the right foot a step towards 1 o'clock, straightening the left leg with the whole foot on the floor and bending the right leg at the knee. At the same time, with the body turning slightly to the right, gradually raise the right hand to eye level with the palm facing obliquely upward and elbow slightly bent, and press the left hand down to the side of the left hip, palm down. Look at the right hand (Fig. 6-22, Fig. 6-23).

⑤ 与③动作相同，只是左右相反（图6-24至图6-26）。

Repeat movements in ③, reversing "right" and "left" (Fig. 6-24 to Fig. 6-26).

⑥ 与④动作相同，只是左右相反（图6-27、图6-28）。

Repeat movements in ④, reversing "right" and "left" (Fig. 6-27, Fig. 6-28).

 图 6-22 （Fig. 6-22）
 图 6-23 （Fig. 6-23）
 图 6-24 （Fig. 6-24）
 图 6-25 （Fig. 6-25）

 图 6-26 （Fig. 6-26）
 图 6-27 （Fig. 6-27）
 图 6-28 （Fig. 6-28）

要点：上体不可前俯后仰，胸部必须宽松舒展。两臂分开时要保持弧形。身体转动时要以腰为轴。弓步动作与分手动作的速度要均匀一致。做弓步时，迈出的脚先是脚跟着地，然后脚掌慢慢踏实，脚尖向前，膝盖不要超过脚尖，后腿自然伸直，前后脚夹角约成 45°～60°（需要时后脚脚跟可以后蹬调整）。野马分鬃式的弓步，前后脚的脚跟要分在中

Points to Remember：Hold torso erect and keep chest relaxed. Move arms in a curve without stretching them when you separate hands using waist as the axis in the body turns. The movements in taking a bow stance and separating hands must be smooth and synchronized in tempo. When taking a bow stance. Place the front foot slowly in position with heel coming down first The knee of the front leg should not go beyond toes while the rear leg should be straightened, form-

轴线两侧，它们之间的横向距离（即以动作行进的中线为纵轴，其两侧的垂直距离为横向）应该保持在10～30厘米左右。

ing an angle of 45-60 degrees with the ground. There should be a transverse distance of 10-30 cm between heels.

三　白鹤亮翅

① 上体微向左转，左手翻掌向下，左臂平屈胸前，右手向左上划弧，手心转向上，与左手成抱球状；眼看左手（图6-29）。

② 右脚跟进半步，上体后坐，身体重心移至右腿，上体先向右转，面向右前方，眼看右手；然后左脚稍向前移，脚尖点地，成左虚步，同时上体再微向左转，面向前方，两手随转体慢慢向右上左下分开，右手上提停于右额前，手心向左后方，左手落于左胯前，手心向下，指尖向前；眼平看前方（图6-30、图6-31）。

3　White crane spread its wing

① With the body turning slightly to the left, make a hold-ball gesture in front of the left part of the chest with the left hand on top. Look at the left hand (Fig. 6-29).

② Draw the right foot half a step towards the left foot and then sit back. Turn the body slightly to the right with weight shifted onto the right leg and eyes looking at the right hand. Move the left foot a bit forward, with toes on the floor for a left "empty stance" with both legs slightly bent at the knee. At the same time, with the body turning slightly to the left, raise the right hand to the front of the right temple with the palm turned inward; while the left hand moves down to the front of the left hip, and the palm down. Look straight ahead (Fig. 6-30, Fig. 6-31).

图6-29　(Fig. 6-29)

图6-30　(Fig. 6-30)

图6-31　(Fig. 6-31)

要点：完成姿势胸部不要挺出，两臂上下都要保持半圆形，左膝要微屈。身体重心后移和右手上提、左手下按

Points to Remember: Do not thrust chest forward. Arms should be rounded when they move up or down. The left knee slightly bend. Weight transfer should be

要协调一致。

第二组

四 左右搂膝拗步

① 右手从体前下落,由下向后上方划弧至右肩外侧,肘微屈,手与耳同高,手心斜向上;左手由左下向上、向右下方划弧至右胸前,手心斜向下;同时上体先微向左再向右转;左脚收至右脚内侧,脚尖点地,眼看右手(图6-32至图6-34)。

coordinated with the raising of the right hand and the pressing of the left hand.

Group 2

4 Brush knees and twist steps on both sides

① Turn the body slightly to the left (11 o'clock) as the right hand moves down while the left hand moves up. Then turn the body to the right as the right hand circles past abdomen and up to ear level with the arm slightly bent and the palm facing obliquely upward while the left hand moves in an upward, rightward, downward curve to the front of the right part of the chest, the palm facing obliquely downward. Look at the right hand (Fig. 6-32 to Fig. 6-34).

太极拳 第二组

图 6-32 (Fig. 6-32)

图 6-33 (Fig. 6-33)

图 6-34 (Fig. 6-34)

② 上体左转,左脚向前(偏左)迈出成左弓步;同时右手屈回由耳侧向前推出,高与鼻尖平,左手向下由左膝前搂过落于左胯旁,指尖向前;眼看右手手指(图6-35、图6-36)。

② Turn torso to the left as the left foot takes a step in that direction for a left bow stance. At the same time, the right hand draws leftward past the right ear and, following the body turn, pushes forward at nose level with the palm facing forward; while the left hand circles around the left knee to stop beside the left hip, palm down. Look at the fingers of the right hand (Fig. 6-35, Fig. 6-36).

图 6-35 （Fig. 6-35）

图 6-36 （Fig. 6-36）

图 6-37 （Fig. 6-37）

图 6-38 （Fig. 6-38）

图 6-39 （Fig. 6-39）

图 6-40 （Fig. 6-40）

③ 右腿慢慢屈膝，上体后坐，身体重心移至右腿，左脚尖翘起微向外撇，随后脚掌慢慢踏实，左腿前弓，身体左转，身体重心移至左腿，右脚收到左脚内侧，脚尖点地；同时左手向外翻掌由左后向上划弧至左肩外侧，肘微屈，手与耳同高，手心斜向上，右手随转体向上、向左下划弧落于左胸前，手心斜向上，眼看左手（图 6-37 至图 6-39）。

③ Sit back slowly with the right knee bent. Shifting the weight onto the right leg. Raise toes of the left foot and turn them a bit outward before placing the whole foot on the floor. Then bend the left leg slowly and turn the body slightly to the left, shifting weight onto the left leg. Bring the right foot forward to the side of the left foot, toes on the floor. At the same time, turn the left palm up and with elbow slightly bent, move the left hand sideways and up to shoulder level while the right hand following the body turn, moves in an upward, leftward downward curve to the front of the left part of the chest. With the palm facing obliquely downward. Look at the left hand (Fig. 6-37 to Fig. 6-39).

④ 与②动作相同,只是左右相反(图 6-40、图 6-41)。

④ Repeat movements in ②, reversing "right" and "left" (Fig. 6-40, Fig. 6-41).

⑤ 与③动作相同,只是左右相反(图 6-42 至图 6-44)。

⑤ Repeat movements in ③, reversing "right" and "left" (Fig. 6-42 to Fig. 6-44).

图 6-41 (Fig. 6-41)

图 6-42 (Fig. 6-42)

图 6-43 (Fig. 6-43)

⑥ 与②动作相同(图 6-45、图 6-46)。

⑥ Repeat movements in ② (Fig. 6-45, Fig. 6-46).

要点:前手推出时,身体不可前俯后仰,要松腰松胯。推掌时要沉肩垂肘、舒指坐腕,同时须与松腰、弓腿上下协调一致。搂膝拗步成弓步时,两脚跟的横向距离保持约 30 厘米左右。

Points to Remember: When pushing the front palm, the body should not bend forward or backward, but should keep hip and waist relaxed. When pushing hands the shoulders should be kept down and make the wrist down as well as relax the palm. All the above movements should be coincided with a relaxed waist and bent knees totally. when holding the knees and taking the bent step, the distance between heels should be about 30 cm.

五 手挥琵琶

右脚跟进半步,上体后坐,身体重

5 Playing the pipa

Move the right foot half a step towards the left heel. Sit

心转至右腿上，上体半面向右转，左脚略提起稍向前移，变成左虚步，脚跟着地，脚尖翘起，膝部微屈；同时左手由左下向上挑举，高与鼻尖平，掌心向右，臂微屈；右手收回放在左臂肘部里侧，掌心向左；眼看左手食指（图 6-47 至图 6-49）。

back and turn torso slightly to the right (1-2 o'clock), shifting weight onto the right leg. Raise the left foot and place it slightly forward, with heel coining down on the floor and knee bent a little for a left empty stance. At the same time, raise the left hand in a curve to nose level with the palm facing rightward and elbow slightly bent while the right hand moves to the inside of the left elbow with the palm facing leftward. Look at the forefinger of the left hand (Fig. 6-47 to Fig. 6-49).

图 6-44 （Fig. 6-44）

图 6-45 （Fig. 6-45）

图 6-46 （Fig. 6-46）

图 6-47 （Fig. 6-47）

图 6-48 （Fig. 6-48）

图 6-49 （Fig. 6-49）

要点：身体要平稳自然，沉肩垂肘、胸部放松；左手上起时不要直向上挑，要由左向上、向前，微带弧形；右脚跟进时，脚掌先着地，再全脚踏实；身体重心后移和左手上起、右手回收要协调一致。

六　左右倒卷肱

① 上体右转，右手翻掌（手心向上）经腹前由下向后上方划弧平举，臂微屈，左手随即翻掌向上；眼的视线随着向右转体先向右看，再转向前方看左手（图6-50、图6-51）。

Points to Remember: The body position should remain steady and natural with chest relaxed and shoulders and elbows held down. Movements in raising the left hand should be more or less circular. In moving the right foot half a step forward, place it, slowly in position with toes coming down first. Weight transfer must be coordinated with the raising of the left hand and the drawing back of the right hand.

6　Backward steps and swirling arms on both sides

① Turn torso slightly to the right, moving the right hand down in a curve past abdomen and then upward to shoulder level with the palm up and arm slightly bent. Turn the left palm up and place toes of the left foot on the floor. Eyes first look to the right as the body turns in that direction, and then turn to look at the left hand (Fig. 6-50, Fig. 6-51).

图 6-50　（Fig. 6-50）

图 6-51　（Fig. 6-51）

② 右臂屈肘折向前，右手由耳侧向前推出，手心向前，左臂屈肘后撤，手心向上，撤至左肋外侧；同时左腿轻轻提起向后（偏左）退一步，脚掌先着地，然后全脚慢慢踏实，身体重心移到左腿上，成右虚步，右脚随转体以脚掌为轴扭正；眼看右手（图6-52、图6-53）。

② Bend the right arm and draw hand past the right ear before pushing it out with the palm facing forward while the left hand moves to the waist side with the palm up. At the same time, raise the left foot slightly and take a curved step backward, placing down toes first and then the whole foot slowly on the floor with toes turned outward. Turn the body slightly to the left and shift weight onto the left leg for a right empty stance, with the right foot pivoting on toes until it points directly ahead. Look at the right hand (Fig. 6-52, Fig. 6-53).

③ 上体微向左转，同时左手随转体向后上方划弧平举，手心向上，右手随即翻掌，掌心向上；眼随转体先向左看，再转向前方看右手（图6-54）。

③ Turn torso slightly to the left, carrying the left hand sideways up to shoulder level with the palm up while the right palm is turned up. Eyes look to the left as the body turns in that direction and then turn to look at the right hand (Fig. 6-54).

图 6-52 (Fig. 6-52)

图 6-53 (Fig. 6-53)

图 6-54 (Fig. 6-54)

④ 与②动作相同，只是左右相反（图6-55、图6-56）。

④ Repeat movements in ②, reversing "right" and "left" (Fig. 6-55, Fig. 6-56).

⑤ 与③动作相同，只是左右相反（图6-57）。

⑤ Repeat movements in ③, reversing "right" and "left" (Fig. 6-57).

⑥ 与②动作相同（图6-58、图6-59）。

⑥ Repeat movements in ② (Fig. 6-58, Fig. 6-59).

⑦ 与③动作相同（图6-60）。

⑦ Repeat movements in ③ (Fig. 6-60).

⑧ 与②动作相同，只是左右相反（图6-61、图6-62）。

⑧ Repeat movements in ②, reversing "right" and "left" (Fig. 6-61, Fig. 6-62).

要点：前推的手不要伸直，后撤手也不可直向回抽，随转体仍走弧线；前推时，要转腰松胯，两手的速度要一致，避免僵硬；退步时，脚掌先着地，再慢慢全脚踏实，同时，前脚随转体以脚掌

Points to Remember: Hands should move in curves when they are being pushed out or drawn back. While pushing out hands, keep waist and hips relaxed. The turning of the waist should be coordinated with hand movements hen stepping back, place toes down first

为轴扭正。退左脚略向左后斜，退右脚略向右后斜，避免使两脚落在一条直线上；后退时，眼神随转体动作先向左右看，然后再转看前手；最后退右脚时，脚尖外撤的角度略大些，便于接做"左揽雀尾"的动作。

and then slowly set the whole foot on the floor. Simultaneously the body turns, pointing the front foot directly ahead, pivoting on toes. When stepping back, the foot should move a bit sideways so that there will be a transverse distance between heels. First look at the direction of left and right and then turn to look at the hand in front.

图 6-55 （Fig. 6-55）

图 6-56 （Fig. 6-56）

图 6-57 （Fig. 6-57）

图 6-58 （Fig. 6-58）

图 6-59 （Fig. 6-59）

图 6-60 （Fig. 6-60）

图 6-61 (Fig. 6-61)

图 6-62 (Fig. 6-62)

第三组

七 左揽雀尾

太极拳 第三组

① 上体微向右转，同时右手随转体向后上方划弧平举，手心向上，左手放松，手心向下；眼看左手（图 6-63）。

② 身体继续向右转，左手自然下落逐渐翻掌经腹前划弧至右肋前，手心向上；右臂屈时，手心转向下，收至右胸前，两手相对成抱球状；同时身体重心落在右腿上，左脚收到右脚内侧，脚尖点地；眼看右手（图 6-64、图 6-65）。

③ 上体微向左转，左脚向左前方迈出，上体继续向左转，右腿自然蹬直，左腿屈膝，成左弓步；同时左臂向左前方掤出（即左臂平屈成弓形，用前臂外侧和手背向前方推出），高与肩平，手心向后；右手向右下落放于右胯旁，手心向下，指尖向前；眼看左前臂（图 6-66、图 6-67）。

Group 3

7 Grasp the peacock's tail-left style

① Turn body slightly to the right (1-2 o'clock), carrying the right hand sideways up to shoulder level with the palm up, while the left palm is turned downward. Look at the left hand (Fig. 6-63).

② Turn the body slightly to the right (3 o'clock) and make a hold-ball gesture in front of the right part of the chest, the right hand on top. At the same time, shift weight onto the right leg and draw the left foot to the side of the right foot with toes on the floor. Look at the right hand (Fig. 6-64, Fig. 6-65).

③ Turn the body slightly to the left, taking a step forward with the left foot towards 11 o'clock for a left bow stance. Meanwhile, push out the left forearm and the back of the hand up to shoulder level as if to bend off a bow, while the right hand drops slowly to the side of the right hip and palm down. Look at the left forearm (Fig. 6-66, Fig. 6-67).

图 6-63 （Fig. 6-63） 图 6-64 （Fig. 6-64） 图 6-65 （Fig. 6-65）

图 6-66 （Fig. 6-66） 图 6-67 （Fig. 6-67）

要点：掤出时，两臂前后均保持弧形。分手、松腰、弓腿三者必须协调一致。揽雀尾弓步时，两脚跟横向距离不超过10厘米。

Points to Remember：Keep both arms rounded while pushing out one of them. The separation of hands, relaxing of waist and bending of the leg should be co-ordinated. There should be less than a transverse distance of 10 cm between heels when taking a grasping peacock's tail.

④ 身体微向左转，左手随即前伸翻掌向下，右手翻掌向上，经腹前向

④ Turn the body slightly to the left (11 o'clock) while extending the left hand forward with palm

第六章　24式太极拳动作图解　**101**

上、向前伸至左前臂下方；然后两手下捋，即上体向右转，两手经腹前向右后上方划弧，直至右手手心向上，高与肩齐，左臂平屈于胸前，手心向后；同时身体重心移至右腿；眼看右手（图6-68、图6-69）。

down. Bring up the right hand until it is below the left forearm with palm up. Then turn torso slightly to the right while pulling both hands down in a curve past the abdomen until the right hand is extended sideways at shoulder level, palm up, and the left forearm lies across the chest with the palm turned inward. At the same time, shift weight onto the right leg. Look at the right hand. (Fig. 6-68, Fig. 6-69).

图 6-68 （Fig. 6-68）

图 6-69 （Fig. 6-69）

要点：下捋时，上体不可前倾，臀部不要凸出。两臂下捋须随腰旋转，仍走弧线。左脚全掌着地。

Points to Remember: While pulling down hands, do not lean forward or protrude buttocks. Arms should follow the turning of the waist and move in a circular path. Set the left foot on the ground.

⑤ 上体微向左转，右臂屈肘折回，右手附于左手腕里侧（相距约5厘米），上体继续向左转，双手同时向前慢慢挤出，左手心向后，右手心向前，左前臂要保持半圆；同时身体重心逐渐前移变成左弓步；眼看左手腕部（图6-70、图6-71）。

⑤ Turn torso slightly to the left as you bend the right arm and place the right hand inside the left wrist; turn torso further to 9 o'clock as you press both hands slowly forward, palms facing each other and keeping a distance of about 5 cm between them and the left arm remaining round. Meanwhile, shift weight slowly onto the left leg for a left bow stance. Look at the left wrist (Fig. 6-70, Fig. 6-71).

要点：向前挤时，上体要正直。挤的动作要与松腰、弓腿相一致。

Points to Remember: Keep torso erect when pressing hands forward. The movement of hands must be coordinated with the relaxing of the waist and bending of the front leg.

图 6-70 (Fig. 6-70)

图 6-71 (Fig. 6-71)

图 6-72 (Fig. 6-72)

⑥ 左手翻掌，手心向下，右手经左腕上方向前、向右伸出，高与左手齐，手心向下，两手左右分开，与肩同宽；然后右腿屈膝，上体慢慢后坐，身体重心移至右腿上，左脚尖不能翘起；同时两手屈肘回收至腹前，手心均向前下方；眼向前平看（图6-72至图6-74）。

⑥ Turn both palms downward as the right hand passes over the left wrist and moves forward and then to the right until it is on the same level with the left hand. Separate hands shoulder-width apart and draw them back to the front of the abdomen with palms facing obliquely downward. At the same time, sit back and shift weight onto the right leg which is slightly bent, raising toes of the left foot. Look straight ahead (Fig. 6-72 to Fig. 6-74).

图 6-73 (Fig. 6-73)

图 6-74 (Fig. 6-74)

图 6-75 (Fig. 6-75)

⑦ 身体重心慢慢前移，同时两手向前、向上按出，掌心向前；左腿前弓成左弓步；眼平看前方（图6-75）。

要点：向前按时，两手须走曲线，手腕部高与肩平，两肘微屈。

八 右揽雀尾

① 上体后坐并向右转，身体重心移至右腿，左脚尖里扣；右手向右平行划弧至右侧，然后由下经腹前向左上划弧至左肋前，手心向上；左臂平屈胸前，左手掌向下与右手成抱球状；同时身体重心再移至左腿上，右脚收至左脚内侧，脚尖点地；眼看左手（图6-76至图6-79）。

⑦ Transfer weight slowly onto the left leg while pushing palms in an upward, forward curve until wrists are the same level with shoulders. At the same time, bend the left leg for a left bow stance. Look straight ahead (Fig. 6-75).

Points to Remember: When pushing hands, it should do circle line and wrists keep as high as shoulders. The elbows bend slightly.

8 Grasp the peacock's tail-right style

① Sit back and turn torso to the right, shifting weight onto the right leg and turning toes of the left foot inward. Move the right hand in a horizontal curve to the right and then in a downward curve past the abdomen for a hold-ball gesture in front of the left part of the chest with the left hand on top. Meanwhile, shift weight onto the left leg and place the right foot beside the left foot then toes on the floor. Look at the left hand (Fig. 6-76 to Fig. 6-79).

图6-76 (Fig. 6-76)　　图6-77 (Fig. 6-77)　　图6-78 (Fig. 6-78)

② 上体微向右转，右脚向右前方迈出，上体继续向右转，左腿自然蹬直，右腿屈膝，成右弓步；同时右臂向右前方掤出（即右臂平屈成弓形，用前臂外侧和手背向前方推出），高与肩平，

② Turn the body slightly to the right, taking a step forward with the right foot towards 3 o'clock for a right bow stance. Meanwhile, push out the right forearm and the back of the hand up to shoulder level as if to bend off a bow, while the left hand drops slowly

手心向后；左手向左下落放于左胯旁，手心向下，指尖向前；眼看右前臂（图6-80、图6-81）。

to the side of the left hip and palm down. Look at the right forearm.（Fig. 6-80，Fig. 6-81）.

图 6-79 （Fig. 6-79）　　　图 6-80 （Fig. 6-80）　　　图 6-81 （Fig. 6-81）

要点：掤出时，两臂前后均保持弧形。分手、松腰、弓腿三者必须协调一致。揽雀尾弓步时，两脚跟横向距离不超过10厘米。

Points to Remember：Keep both arms round while pushing out one of them. The separation of hands, relaxing of waist and bending of leg should be coordinated. There should be less than a transverse distance of 10 cm between heels when taking a grasping peacock's tail.

③ 身体微向右转，右手随即前伸翻掌向下，左手翻掌向上，经腹前向上、向前伸至右前臂下方；然后两手下捋，上体向左转，两手经腹前向左后上方划弧，直至左手手心向上，高与肩齐，右臂平屈于胸前，手心向后；同时身体重心移至左腿；眼看左手（图6-82、图6-83）。

③ Turn the body slightly to the right while extending the right hand forward with palm down. Bring up the left hand until it is below the right forearm with palm up. Then turn torso slightly to the left while pulling both hands down in a curve past the abdomen until the left hand is extended sideways at shoulder level, palm up, and the right forearm lies across the chest with the palm turned inward. At the same time, shift weight onto the left leg. Look at the left hand（Fig. 6-82，Fig. 6-83）.

要点：下捋时，上体不可前倾，臀部不要凸出。两臂下捋须随腰旋转，仍走弧线。右脚全掌着地。

Points to Remember：While pulling down hands, do not lean forward or protrude buttocks. Arms should follow the turning of the waist and move in a circular path. Set the right foot on the ground.

图 6-82 （Fig. 6-82）　　　图 6-83 （Fig. 6-83）

④ 上体微向右转，左臂屈肘折回，左手附于右手腕里侧（相距约5厘米），上体继续向右转，双手同时向前慢慢挤出，右手心向后，左手心向前，右前臂要保持半圆；同时身体重心逐渐前移变成右弓步；眼看右手腕部（图6-84、图6-85）。

④ Turn torso slightly to the right as you bend the left arm and place the left hand inside the right wrist; turn torso further to 3 o'clock as you press both hands slowly forward, palms facing each other and keeping a distance of about 5 cm between them and the right arm remaining round. Meanwhile, shift weight slowly onto the right leg for a right bow stance. Look at the right wrist （Fig. 6-84，Fig. 6-85）.

图 6-84 （Fig. 6-84）　　　图 6-85 （Fig. 6-85）　　　图 6-86 （Fig. 6-86）

要点：向前挤时，上体要正直。挤的动作要与松腰、弓腿相一致。

⑤ 右手翻掌，手心向下，左手经左腕上方向前、向左伸出，高与右手齐，手心向下，两手左右分开，宽与肩同；然后左腿屈膝，上体慢慢后坐，身体重心移至左腿上，右脚尖不能翘起；同时两手屈肘回收至腹前，手心均向前下方；眼向前平看（图6-86至图6-88）。

⑥ 上式不停，身体重心慢慢前移，同时两手向前、向上按出，掌心向前；右腿前弓成右弓步；眼平看前方（图6-89）。

Points to Remember: Keep torso erect when pressing hands forward. The movement of hands must be coordinated with the relaxing of the waist and bending of the front leg.

⑤ Turn both palms downward as the left hand passes over the right wrist and moves forward and then to the left until it is on the same level with the right hand. Separate hands shoulder-width apart and draw them back to the front of the abdomen with palms facing obliquely downward. At the same time, sit back and shift weight onto the left leg which is slightly bent, raising toes of the right foot. Look straight ahead (Fig. 6-86 to Fig. 6-88).

⑥ Transfer weight slowly onto the right leg while pushing palms in an upward, forward curve until wrists are the same level with shoulders. At the same time, bend the right leg for a right bow stance. Look straight ahead (Fig. 6-89).

图 6-87 （Fig. 6-87）

图 6-88 （Fig. 6-88）

图 6-89 （Fig. 6-89）

要点：向前按时，两手须走曲线，手腕部高与肩平，两肘微屈。

Points to Remember: When pushing hands, it should do circle line and wrists keep as high as shoulders. The elbows bend slightly.

第四组

九 单鞭

① 上体后坐，身体重心逐渐移至

Group 4

9 Single whip

① Sit back and shift weight gradually

左脚上，右脚尖里扣；同时上体左转，两手（左高右低）向左弧形运转，直至左臂平举，伸于身体左侧，手心向左，右手经腹前运至左肋前，手心向后上方；眼看左手（图6-90、图6-91）。

onto the left leg, turning toes of the right foot inward. Meanwhile, turn the body to the left, carrying both hands leftward with the left hand on top until the left arm is extended sideways at shoulder level that with the palm facing outward, and the right hand is in front of the left ribs with the palm facing obliquely inward. Look at the left hand (Fig. 6-90, Fig. 6-91).

② 身体重心再渐渐移至右腿上，上体右转，左脚向右脚靠拢，脚尖点地；同时右手向右上方划弧（手心由里转向外），至右侧方时变勾手，臂与肩平；左手向下经腹前向右上划弧停于右肩前，手心向里；眼看左手（图6-92、图6-93）。

② Turn the body to the right, shifting weight gradually onto the right leg and drawing the left foot to the side of the right foot, with toes on the floor. At the same time, move the right hand up to the right until arm is at shoulder level. With the right palm now turned outward, bunch fingertips and turn them downward from wrist for a "hook hand", while the left hand moves in a curve past abdomen up to the front of the right shoulder with palm facing inward, Look at the left hand (Fig. 6-92, Fig. 6-93).

图 6-90 （Fig. 6-90）

图 6-91 （Fig. 6-91）

图 6-92 （Fig. 6-92）

③ 上体微向左转，左脚向左前侧方迈出，右脚跟后蹬，成左弓步；在身体重心移向左腿的同时，左掌随上体的继续左转慢慢翻转向前推出，手心向前，手指与眼齐平，臂微屈；眼看左手（图6-94、图6-95）。

③ Turn the body to the left while the left foot takes a step towards 10-11 o'clock for a left bow stance. While shifting weight onto the left leg, turn the left palm slowly outward, as you push it forward with fingertips at eye level and elbow slightly bent. Look at the left hand (Fig. 6-94, Fig. 6-95).

图 6-93 （Fig. 6-93）　　图 6-94 （Fig. 6-94）　　图 6-95 （Fig. 6-95）

要点：上体保持正直，松腰；完成式时，右臂肘部稍下垂，左肘与左膝上下相对，两肩下沉；左手向外翻掌前推时，要随转体边翻边推出，不要翻掌太快或最后突然翻掌；全部过渡动作，上下要协调一致。

Points to Remember: Keep torso erect, with waist relaxed and shoulders lowered. The left palm is turned outward slowly, not too abruptly as hand pushes forward. All transitional movements must be well-coordinated. Face 9 o'clock in the final position, with the right elbow slightly bent downward and the left elbow above the left knee directly.

十　云手

① 身体重心移至右腿上，身体渐向右转，左脚尖里扣；左手经腹前向右上划弧至右肩前，手心斜向后，同时右手变掌，手心向右前；眼看左手（图6-96至图6-98）。

② 上体慢慢左转，身体重心随之逐渐左移；左手由脸前向左侧运转，手心渐渐转向左方；右手由右下经腹前向左上划弧，至左肩前，手心斜向后；同时右脚靠近左脚，成小开立步（两脚距离约10～20厘米）；眼看右手（图6-99、图6-100）。

10　Wave Hands Like Clouds

① Shift weight onto the right leg and turn the body gradually to the right turning toes of the left foot inward. At the same time, move the left hand in a curve past abdomen to the front of the right shoulder, then the palm turned obliquely inward; while the right hand is opened, the palm facing outward. Look at the left hand (Fig. 6-96 to Fig. 6-98).

② Turn torso gradually to the left, shifting weight onto the left leg. At the same time, move the left hand in a curve past face with palm turned slowly leftward, while the right hand moves in a curve past abdomen up to the front of the left shoulder with the palm slowly turning obliquely inward. As the right hand moves upward, bring the right foot to the side of the left foot so that they are parallel and 10-20 cm apart. Look at the right hand (Fig. 6-99, Fig. 6-100).

图 6-96 （Fig. 6-96）

图 6-97 （Fig. 6-97）

图 6-98 （Fig. 6-98）

图 6-99 （Fig. 6-99）

图 6-100 （Fig. 6-100）

③ 上体再向右转，同时左手经腹前向右上划弧至右肩前，手心斜向后；右手向右侧运转，手心翻转向右；随之左脚向左横跨一步；眼看左手（图 6-101 至图 6-103）。

③ Turn torso gradually to the right, shifting weight onto the right leg. At the same time, move the right hand continuously to the right side past face, with the palm turned slowly outward, while the left hand moves in a curve past abdomen up to shoulder level with the palm turned slowly obliquely inward. As the left hand moves upward, take a side step with the left foot. Look at the left hand （Fig. 6-101 to Fig. 6-103）.

图 6-101 （Fig. 6-101）

图 6-102 （Fig. 6-102）

图 6-103 （Fig. 6-103）

④ 上体慢慢左转，身体重心随之逐渐左移；左手由脸前向左侧运转，手心渐渐转向左方；右手由右下经腹前向左上划弧，至左肩前，手心斜向后；同时右脚靠近左脚，成小开立步（两脚距离约 10～20 厘米）；眼看右手（图 6-104、图 6-105）。

④ Turn torso gradually to the left, shifting weight onto the left leg. At the same time, move the left hand in a curve past face with palm turned slowly leftward, while the right hand moves in a curve past abdomen up to the front of the left shoulder with the palm slowly turning obliquely inward. As the right hand moves upward, bring the right foot to the side of the left foot so that they are parallel and 10-20 cm apart. Look at the right hand (Fig. 6-104, Fig. 6-105).

图 6-104 （Fig. 6-104）

图 6-105 （Fig. 6-105）

⑤ 上体再向右转，同时左手经腹前向右上划弧至右肩前，手心斜向后；右手向右侧运转，手心翻转向右；随之左脚向左横跨一步；眼看左手（图6-106至图6-108）。

⑤ Turn torso gradually to the right, shifting weight onto the right leg. At the same time, move the right hand continuously to the right side past face, with the palm turned slowly outward, while the left hand moves in a curve past abdomen up to shoulder level with the palm turned slowly obliquely inward. As the left hand moves upward, take a side step with the left foot. Look at the left hand（Fig. 6-106 to Fig. 6-108）.

图 6-106 （Fig. 6-106）

图 6-107 （Fig. 6-107）

图 6-108 （Fig. 6-108）

⑥ 上体慢慢左转，身体重心随之逐渐左移；左手由脸前向左侧运转，手心渐渐转向左方；右手由右下经腹前向左上划弧，至左肩前，手心斜向后；同时右脚靠近左脚，成小开立步（两脚距离约10～20厘米）；眼看右手（图6-109、图6-110）。

⑥ Turn torso gradually to the left, shifting weight onto the left leg. At the same time, move the left hand in a curve past face with palm turned slowly leftward, while the right hand moves in a curve past abdomen up to the front of the left shoulder with the palm slowly turning obliquely inward. As the right hand moves upward, bring the right foot to the side of the left foot so that they are parallel and 10-20 cm apart. Look at the right hand (Fig. 6-109, Fig. 6-110).

要点：身体转动要以腰脊为轴，松腰、松胯，不可忽高忽低；两臂随腰的转动而运转，要自然圆活，速度要缓慢均匀；下肢移动时，身体重心要稳定，两脚掌先着地再踏实，脚尖向前；眼的视线随左右手而移动；第三个"云手"，右脚最后跟步时，脚尖微向里扣，便于接"单鞭"动作。

Points to Remember: Use your lumbar spine as the axis when the body turns. Keep the waist and hips relaxed. Do not let your body rise and fall abruptly. Arm movements should be natural and circular and follow waist movements. Pace must be slow and even. Maintain a good balance when moving lower limbs. Eyes should follow the hand that is moving.

图 6-109　(Fig. 6-109)

图 6-110　(Fig. 6-110)

十一　单鞭

① 上体向右转，右手随之向右运转，至右侧方时变成勾手；左手经腹前向右上划弧至右肩前，手心向内；身体重心落在右腿上，左脚尖点地；眼看左手（图 6-111 至图 6-113）。

11　Single whip

① Turn torso to the right, moving the right hand to the right side for a hook hand while the left hand moves in a curve past the abdomen to the front of the right shoulder with the palm turned inward. Shift weight onto the right leg with toes of the left foot on the floor. Look at the left hand（Fig. 6-111 to Fig. 6-113）.

图 6-111　(Fig. 6-111)

图 6-112　(Fig. 6-112)

图 6-113　(Fig. 6-113)

第六章　24 式太极拳动作图解

②上体微向左转，左脚向左前侧方迈出，右脚跟后蹬，成左弓步；在身体重心移向左腿的同时，上体继续左转，左掌慢慢翻转向前推出，成"单鞭"式（图6-114、图6-115）。

② Turn the body to the left while the left foot takes a step towards 10-11 o'clock for a left bow stance. While shifting weight onto the left leg, turn the left palm slowly outward, as you push it forward with fingertips at eye level and elbow slightly bent. Look at the left hand（Fig. 6-114，Fig. 6-115）.

图 6-114 （Fig. 6-114）

图 6-115 （Fig. 6-115）

要点：上体保持正直，松腰；完成式时，右臂肘部稍下垂，左肘与左膝上下相对，两肩下沉；左手向外翻掌前推时，要随转体边翻边推出，不要翻掌太快或最后突然翻掌；全部过渡动作，上下要协调一致。

Points to Remember：Keep torso erect, with waist relaxed and shoulders lowered. The left palm is turned outward slowly, not too abruptly as hand pushes forward. All transitional movements must be well-coordinated. Face 9 o'clock in the final position, with the right elbow slightly bent downward and the left elbow above the left knee directly.

第五组

十二　高探马

①右脚跟进半步，身体重心逐渐后移至右腿上；右勾手变成掌，两手心翻转向上，两肘微屈；同时身体微向右转，左脚跟渐渐离地；眼看左前方（图6-116）。

②上体微向左转，面向前方；右

Group 5

12　High pat on horse

① Draw the right foot half a step forward and shift weight gradually onto the right leg. Open the right hand and turn up both palms, elbows slightly bent, while the body turns slightly to the right, raising the left heel gradually for a left empty stance. Look at the left hand (Fig. 6-116).

② Turn the body slightly to the left, pushing the

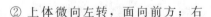
太极拳　第五组

掌经右耳旁向前推出，手心向前，手指与眼同高；左手收至左侧腰前，手心向上；同时左脚微向前移，脚尖点地，成左虚步；眼看右手（图6-117）。

right palm forward past the right ear, fingertips at eye level. while the left hand moves to the front of the left hip and palm up. At the same time, move the left foot a bit forward for a left empty step with toes on the floor. Look at the right hand (Fig. 6-117).

图 6-116　（Fig. 6-116）

图 6-117　（Fig. 6-117）

要点：上体自然正直，双肩要下沉，右肘微下垂。

Points to Remember: Keep torso erect, shoulders lowered and the right elbow slightly downward.

十三　右蹬脚

① 左手手心向上，前伸至右手腕背面，两手相互交叉，随即向两侧分开并向下划弧，手心斜向下；同时左脚提起向左前侧方进步（脚尖略外撇）；身体重心前移，右腿自然蹬直，成左弓步；眼看前方（图6-118至图6-120）。

② 两手由外圈向里圈划弧，两手交叉合抱于胸前，右手在外，手心均向里，同时右脚向左脚靠拢，脚尖点地；眼平看右前方（图6-121）。

13　Kick with the right heel

① Turn torso slightly to the right and move the left hand, palm up, to cross the right hand at the wrist. Then separate hands, moving both in a downward curve with palms turned obliquely downward. Meanwhile, raise the left foot to take a step towards 11 o'clock for a left bow stance then toes turned slightly outward. Look straight ahead (Fig. 6-118 to Fig. 6-120).

② Continue to move hands in a downward, inward, upward curve until wrists cross in front of the chest with the right hand in front and both palms turned inward. At the same time, draw the right foot to the side of the left foot with toes on the floor. Look forward to the right (Fig. 6-121).

图 6-118　(Fig. 6-118)

图 6-119　(Fig. 6-119)

图 6-120　(Fig. 6-120)

③ 两臂左右划弧分开平举，肘部微屈，手心均向外；同时右腿屈膝提起，右脚向右前方慢慢蹬出；眼看右手（图 6-122、图 6-123）。

③ Separate hands, turning torso slightly to 11 o'clock and extending both arms sideways at shoulder level with elbows slightly bent and palms turned outward. At the same time, raise the right knee and thrust foot gradually towards 12 o'clock. Look at the right hand (Fig. 6-122, Fig. 6-123).

图 6-121　(Fig. 6-121)

图 6-122　(Fig. 6-122)

图 6-123　(Fig. 6-123)

要点：身体要稳定，不可前俯后仰。两手分开时，腕部与肩齐平。蹬脚时，左腿微屈，右脚尖回勾，劲使在脚跟。分手和蹬脚须协调一致。右臂和右腿上下相对。

Points to Remember：Keep your balance. Wrists are at shoulder level hen hands are separated. When kicking the right foot, the left leg is slightly bent and the kicking force should be focused on the heel with ankle dorsiflexed. The separation of hands should be coordinated with the kick. The right arm is parallel with the right leg.

十四 双峰贯耳

① 右腿收回，屈膝平举，左手由后向上、向前下落至体前，两手心均翻转向上，两手同时向下划弧分落于右膝盖两侧；眼看前方（图6-124、图6-125）。

14 Striking ears with both fists

① Pull back the right foot and keep the thigh level. Move the left hand in a curve to the side of the right hand in front of chest with both palms turned inward. Bring both hands to either side of the right knee with the palm up. Look straight ahead（Fig. 6-124，Fig. 6-125）.

图 6-124 （Fig. 6-124）   图 6-125 （Fig. 6-125）

② 右脚向右前方落下，身体重心渐渐前移，成右弓步，面向右前方；同时两手下落，慢慢变拳，分别从两侧向上、向前划弧至面部前方，成钳形状，两拳相对，高与耳齐，拳眼都斜向内下（两拳中间距离约10～20厘米）；眼看右拳（图6-126、图6-127）。

② Set the right foot slowly on the floor towards 1 o'clock, shifting weight onto the right leg for a right bow stance. At the same time, lower hands to both sides and gradually clench fists; then move them backward with an inward rotation of the arms before moving them upward and forward for a pincer movement that ends at eye level with fists 10-20 cm apart, knuckles pointing upward to the back. Look at the right fist（Fig. 6-126，Fig. 6-127）.

图 6-126　(Fig. 6-126)　　　图 6-127　(Fig. 6-127)

要点：完成式时，头颈正直，松腰松胯，两拳松握，沉肩垂肘，两臂均保持弧形。

十五　转身左蹬脚

① 左腿屈膝后坐，身体重心移至左腿，上体左转，右脚尖里扣；同时两拳变掌，由上向左右划弧分开平举，手心向前，眼看左手（图 6-128、图 6-129）。

② 身体重心再移至右腿，左脚收到右脚内侧，脚尖点地；同时两手由外圈向里圈划弧合抱于胸前，左手在外，手心均向后；眼平看左方（图 6-130、图 6-131）。

③ 两臂左右划弧分开平举，肘部微屈，手心均向外；同时左腿屈膝提起，左脚向左前方慢慢蹬出；眼看左手（图 6-132、图 6-133）。

Points to Remember：Hold head and neck erect. Keep waist and hips relaxed and fist loosely clenched. Keep shoulders and elbows lowered and arms rounded.

15　Body turning and left heel kicking

① Shift weight gradually onto the left leg, turning the body to the left (9 o'clock) with toes of the right foot turned inward. Simultaneously, open both fists and separate hands in an upward curve and extending both arms sideways with palms facing forward. Look at the left hand (Fig. 6-128, Fig. 6-129).

② Shift weight onto the right leg and draw the left foot to the side of the right foot with toes on the floor. At the same time, move both hands in a downward, inward, upward curve until wrists cross in front of the chest with the left hand in front and both palms facing inward. Look forward to the left (Fig. 6-130, Fig. 6-131).

③ Separate hands, extending both arms sideways at shoulder level with elbows slightly bent and palms facing outward. Meanwhile, raise the left knee and thrust foot gradually towards 10 o'clock. Look at the left hand (Fig. 6-132, Fig. 6-133).

图 6-128 （Fig. 6-128）

图 6-129 （Fig. 6-129）

图 6-130 （Fig. 6-130）

图 6-131 （Fig. 6-131）

图 6-132 （Fig. 6-132）

图 6-133 （Fig. 6-133）

要点：身体要稳定，不可前俯后仰。两手分开时，腕部与肩齐平。蹬脚时，右腿微屈，左脚尖回勾，劲使在脚跟。分手和蹬脚须协调一致。左臂和左腿上下相对。

Points to Remember：Keep your balance. Wrists are at shoulder level hen hands are separated. When kicking the left foot，the right leg is slightly bent and the kicking force should be focused on the heel with ankle dorsiflexed. The separation of hands should be coordinated with the kick. The left arm is parallel with the left leg.

第六组

十六　左下势独立

① 左腿收回平屈，上体右转；右掌变成勾手，左掌向上、向右划弧下落，立于右肩前，掌心斜向后；眼看右手（图6-134、图6-135）。

太极拳　第六组

Group 6

16　Push down and stand on the left foot

① Pull back the left foot and keep the thigh level. Turn torso to the right. Hook the right hand as you move the left arm in a curve past face to the front of the right shoulder, turning it inward in the process. Look at the right hand (Fig. 6-134, Fig. 6-135).

图 6-134　(Fig. 6-134)

图 6-135　(Fig. 6-135)

② 右腿慢慢屈膝下蹲，左腿由内向左侧（偏后）伸出，成左仆步；左手下落（掌心向外）向左下顺左腿内侧向前穿出；眼看左手（图6-136、图6-137）。

要点：右腿全蹲时，上体不可过于前倾。左腿伸直，左脚尖须向里扣，两脚脚掌全部着地。左脚尖与右脚跟踏在中轴线上。

③ 身体重心前移，左脚跟为轴，脚尖尽量向外撇，左腿前弓，右腿后蹬，

② Turn torso to the left, and crouch down slowly on the right leg, stretching the left leg sideways towards 8-9 o'clock. Move the left hand down and to the left along the inner side of the left leg, turning the palm outward. Look at the left hand (Fig. 6-136, Fig. 6-137).

Points to Remember: When crouching down, straighten the left leg with toes turned slightly inward with both soles flat on the floor. Keep toes of the left foot in line with the right heel. Do not lean torso too much forward.

③ Turn toes of the left foot outward and those of the right foot inward; straighten the right leg and bend

图 6-136 （Fig. 6-136）

图 6-137 （Fig. 6-137）

右脚尖里扣，上体微向左转并向前起身；同时左臂继续向前伸出（立掌），掌心向右，右勾手下落，勾尖向后；眼看左手（图 6-138）。

the left leg onto which weight is shifted Turn torso slightly to the left as you rise up slowly in a forward movement. At the same time, move the left arm continuously to the front and palm facing right, while the right hand drops behind the back, still in the form of a hook with bunched fingertips pointing backward. Look at the left hand （Fig. 6-138）.

图 6-138 （Fig. 6-138）

图 6-139 （Fig. 6-139）

图 6-140 （Fig. 6-140）

④ 右腿慢慢提起平屈，成左独立式；同时右勾手变掌，并由后下方顺右腿外侧向前弧形摆出，屈臂立于右腿上方，肘与膝相对，手心向左；左手落于左胯旁，手心向下，指尖向前；眼看右手（图6-139、图6-140）。

要点：上体要正直，独立的腿要微屈，右腿提起时脚尖自然下垂。

十七　右下势独立

① 右脚下落于左脚前，脚掌着地，然后以左脚前掌为轴脚跟转动，身体随之左转，同时左手向后平举变成勾手，右掌随着转体向左侧划弧，立于左肩前，掌心斜向后；眼看左手（图6-141、图6-142）。

④ Raise the right knee slowly as the right hand opens into a palm and swings to the front past outside of the right leg with elbow bent just above the right knee, fingers pointing up and a palm facing left. Move the left hand down to the side of the left hip with the palm down. Look at the right hand (Fig. 6-139, Fig. 6-140).

Points to Remember: Keep torso upright. Bend the supporting leg slightly. Toes of the raised leg should naturally downward.

17　Push down and stand on the right foot

① Put the right foot down in front of the left foot with toes on the floor. Turn the body to the left, pivoting on toes of the left foot. At the same time, raise the left hand sideways to shoulder level and turn it into a hook while the right hand, following the body turn, moves in a curve to the front of the left shoulder with fingers pointing up. Look at the left hand (Fig. 6-141, Fig. 6-142).

图 6-141　(Fig. 6-141)

图 6-142　(Fig. 6-142)

② 左腿慢慢屈膝下蹲，右腿由内向右侧（偏后）伸出，成右仆步；右手下落（掌心向外）向右下顺右腿内侧向前穿出；眼看右手（图6-143、图6-144）。

② Turn torso to the right, and crouch down slowly on the left leg, stretching the right leg sideways towards 3-4 o'clock. Move the right hand down and to the right along the inner side of the right leg, turning the palm outward. Look at the right hand (Fig. 6-143, Fig. 6-144).

要点：左腿全蹲时，上体不可过于前倾。右腿伸直，右脚尖须向里扣，两脚脚掌全部着地。右脚尖与左脚跟踏在中轴线上。

Points to Remember: When crouching down, straighten the right leg with toes turned slightly inward with both soles flat on the floor. Keep toes of the right foot in line with the left heel. Do not lean torso too much forward.

图 6-143 （Fig. 6-143）

图 6-144 （Fig. 6-144）

③ 身体重心前移，右脚跟为轴，脚尖尽量向外撇，右腿前弓，左腿后蹬，左脚尖里扣，上体微向右转并向前起身；同时右臂继续向前伸出（立掌），掌心向左，左勾手下落，勾尖向后；眼看右手（图 6-145）。

③ Turn toes of the right foot outward and those of the left foot inward; straighten the left leg and bend the right leg onto which weight is shifted Turn torso slightly to the right as you rise up slowly in a forward movement. At the same time, move the right arm continuously to the front and palm facing left, while the left hand drops behind the back, still in the form of a hook with bunched fingertips pointing backward. Look at the right hand (Fig. 6-145).

④ 左腿慢慢提起平屈，成右独立式；同时左勾手变掌，并由后下方顺左腿外侧向前弧形摆出，屈臂立于左腿上方，肘与膝相对，手心向右；右手落于右胯旁，手心向下，指尖向前；眼看左手（图 6-146、图 6-147）。

④ Raise the left knee slowly as the left hand opens into a palm and swings to the front past outside of the left leg with elbow bent just above the left knee, fingers pointing up and a palm facing right. Move the right hand down to the side of the right hip with the palm down. Look at the left hand (Fig. 6-146, Fig. 6-147).

要点：右脚尖触地后必须稍微提起，然后再向下仆腿。其他均与"左下势独立"相同，只是左右相反。

Points to Remember: Raise the right foot slightly before crouching down and stretching the right leg sideways. Other points are the same as those for Push down and stand on the Left Foot. "Push Down and Stand on the Left Foot", except that "right" and "left" are reversed.

图 6-145 （Fig. 6-145）　　图 6-146 （Fig. 6-146）　　图 6-147 （Fig. 6-147）

第七组

十八　左右穿梭

太极拳　第七组

① 身体微向左转，左脚向前落地，脚尖外撇，右脚跟离地，两腿屈膝成半坐盘式；同时两手在左胸前成抱球状（左上右下）；然后右脚收到左脚的内侧，脚尖点地；眼看左前臂（图6-148至图6-150）。

② 身体右转，右脚向右前方迈出，屈膝弓腿，成右弓步；同时右手由脸前向上举并翻掌停在右额前，手心斜向上；左手先向左下再经体前向前推出，高与鼻尖平，手心向前；眼看左手（图6-151至图6-153）。

③ 身体重心略向后移，右脚尖稍向外撇，随即身体重心再移至右腿，左脚跟进，停于右脚内侧，脚尖点地；同

Group 7

18　Working with a shuttle on both sides

① Turn the body to the left （11 o'clock） as you set the left foot on the floor in front of the right foot with toes turned outward. With the right heel slightly raised, bend both knees for a half "cross legged seat". At the same time, make a hold-ball gesture in front of the left part of the chest, the left hand on the top. Then move the right foot to the side of the left foot with toes on the floor. Look at the left forearm (Fig. 6-148 to Fig. 6-150).

② Turn the body to the right as the right foot takes a step forward to the right for a right bow stance. At the same time, move the right hand up to the front of the right temple, and the palm turned obliquely upward, while the left palm moves in a small leftward, downward curve before pushing it out forward and upward to nose level. Look at the left hand (Fig. 6-151 to Fig. 6-153).

③ Turn the body slightly to the right （5 o'clock）, shifting weight slightly backward with toes of the right foot turned a bit outward. Then shift weight back onto

图 6-148 (Fig. 6-148)

图 6-149 (Fig. 6-149)

图 6-150 (Fig. 6-150)

图 6-151 (Fig. 6-151)

图 6-152 (Fig. 6-152)

图 6-153 (Fig. 6-153)

时两手在右胸前成抱球状（右上左下）；眼看右前臂（图6-154、图6-155）。

the right leg and draw the left foot to the side of the right foot with toes on the floor. Meanwhile, make a hold-ball gesture in front of the right part of the chest with the right hand on the top. Look at the right forearm (Fig. 6-154, Fig. 6-155).

图 6-154 （Fig. 6-154）　　图 6-155 （Fig. 6-155）

④ 身体左转，左脚向左前方迈出，屈膝弓腿，成左弓步；同时左手由脸前向上举并翻掌停在左额前，手心斜向上；右手先向右下再经体前向前推出，高与鼻尖平，手心向前；眼看右手（图 6-156 至图 6-158）。

④ Turn the body to the left as the left foot takes a step forward to the left for a left bow stance. At the same time, move the left hand up to the front of the left temple, and the palm turned obliquely upward, while the right palm moves in a small rightward, downward curve before pushing it out forward and upward to nose level. Look at the right hand（Fig. 6-156 to Fig. 6-158）.

图 6-156 （Fig. 6-156）　　图 6-157 （Fig. 6-157）　　图 6-158 （Fig. 6-158）

要点：手推出后，上体不可前俯。手向上举时，防止引肩上耸。一手上举一手前推要与弓腿松腰上下协调一致。做弓步时，两脚跟的横向距离同搂膝拗步式，保持在30厘米左右。

十九　海底针

右脚向前跟进半步，身体重心移至右腿，左脚稍向前移，脚尖点地，成左虚步；同时身体稍向右转，右手下落经体前向后、向上提抽至肩上耳旁，再随身体左转，由右耳旁斜向前下方插出，掌心向左，指尖斜向下；与此同时，左手向前、向下划弧落于左胯旁，手心向下，指尖向前；眼看前下方（图6-159、图6-160）。

Points to Remember：Do not lean forward when pushing hands forward, avoid raise shoulders when moving hands upward. Movements of hands should be coordinated with those of the waist and legs. Keep a transverse distance of about 30 cm between heels in bow stance.

19　Needle to the bottom of the sea

Draw the right foot half a step forward, shift weight onto the right leg and move the left foot a bit forward with toes on the floor for a left turning slightly to empty stance. At the same time with the body turning slightly to the right (4 o'clock) and then to the left (3 o'clock), move the right hand down in front of the body, up to the side of the right ear and then obliquely downward in front of the body with the palm facing left and fingers pointing obliquely downward. while the left hand moves in a forward, downward curve to the side of the left hip, with the palm down. Look at floor ahead (Fig. 6-159，Fig. 6-160).

图6-159　（Fig. 6-159）

图6-160　（Fig. 6-160）

要点：上体不可太前倾，避免低头和臀部外凸，左腿要微屈。

Points to Remember：Do not lean too much forward, Keep head erect and buttocks pulled in. The left leg is slightly bent.

二十　闪通臂

上体稍向右转，左脚向前迈出，屈

20　Flashing the arm

Turn the body slightly to the right (4 o'clock) and

膝弓腿成左弓步；同时右手由体前上提，屈臂上举，停于右额前上方，掌心翻转斜向上，拇指朝下；左手上起经胸前向前推出，高与鼻尖平，手心向前；眼看左手（图6-161至图6-163）。

要点：完成姿势上体自然正直，松腰、松胯；左臂不要完全伸直，背部肌肉要伸展开。推掌、举掌和弓腿动作要协调一致。弓步时，两脚跟横向距离同揽雀尾式（不超过10厘米）。

take a step forward with the left foot for a left bow stance. At the same time, raise the right hand with elbow bent to stop above and in front of the right temple, the palm turned obliquely upward with the thumb pointing down, while the left palm moves a bit upward and then pushes forward at nose level. Look at the left hand (Fig. 6-161 to Fig. 6-163).

Points to Remember: Keep torso erect and waist and hips relaxed. Do not straighten the arm when you push the left palm forward. The movement should be synchronized with the taking of bow stance with your back muscles stretched. Keep a transverse distance of less than 10 cm between heels. Face 3 o'clock in the final position.

图 6-161　(Fig. 6-161)

图 6-162　(Fig. 6-162)

图 6-163　(Fig. 6-163)

第八组

二一　转身搬拦捶

太极拳　第八组

① 上体后坐，身体重心移至右腿上，左脚尖里扣，身体向右后转，然后身体重心再移至左腿上；与此同时，右手随着转体向右、向下（变拳）经腹前划弧至左肋旁，掌心向下；左掌上举于头前，掌心斜向上；眼看前方（图6-164、图6-165）。

Group 8

21　Turn to deflect downwards parry and punch

① Sit back and shift weight onto the right leg. Turn the body to the right (4 o'clock), with toes of the left foot turned inward. Then shift weight again on to the left leg. Simultaneously with the body turn, move the right hand in a rightward downward curve and with fingers clenched into the fist, past abdomen to the side of the left ribs with the palm turned down, while the left hand moves up to the front of the forehead, with the palm turned obliquely upward. Look straight ahead (Fig. 6-164, Fig. 6-165).

图 6-164 (Fig. 6-164)

图 6-165 (Fig. 6-165)

图 6-166 (Fig. 6-166)

图 6-167 (Fig. 6-167)

② 向右转体，右拳经胸前向前翻转撇出，拳心向上；左手落于左胯旁，掌心向下，指向前；同时右脚收回后（不要停顿或脚尖点地），随即向前迈出，脚尖外撇；眼看右拳（图 6-166、图 6-167）。

② Turn the body to the right (3 o'clock), bringing the right fist up and then forward and downward for a backhand punch, while the left hand lowers to the side of the left hip with the palm turned down. At the same time, the right foot draws towards the left foot and, without stopping or touching the floor. It takes a step forward with toes turned outward. Look at the right fist (Fig. 6-166, Fig. 6-167).

③ 身体重心移至右腿上，左脚向前迈一步；左手上起经左侧向前上划弧拦出，掌心向前下方；同时右拳向右划弧收到右腰旁，拳心向上；眼看左手（图 6-168、图 6-169）。

③ Shift weight onto the right leg and take a step forward with the left foot. At the same time, carry with the left hand by moving it sideways and up to the front, and the palm turned slightly downward while the right fist withdraws to the side of the right hip with forearm rotating internally and then externally, so that the fist is turned down and then up again. Look at the left hand (Fig. 6-168, Fig. 6-169).

④ 左腿前弓成左弓步，同时右拳向前打出，拳眼向上，高与胸平，左手附于右前臂里侧；眼看右拳（图 6-170）。

④ Bend the left leg for a left bow stance as you strike out the right fist forward at chest level, turning the eye of fist upward. While the left hand withdraws to the side of the right forearm. Look at the right fist (Fig. 6-170).

图 6-168 （Fig. 6-168）

图 6-169 （Fig. 6-169）

图 6-170 （Fig. 6-170）

要点：右拳不要握得太紧。向前打拳时，右肩随拳略向前引伸，沉肩垂肘，右臂要微屈。弓步时，两脚横向距离同揽雀尾式。

Points to Remember: Clench the right fist loosely. Follow the punch with the right shoulder by extending it a bit forward. Keep shoulders and elbows lowered and the right arm slightly bent.

二二　如封似闭

22　Apparent close-up

① 左手由右腕下向前伸出，右拳变掌，两手手心逐渐翻转向上并慢慢分开回收；同时身体后坐，左脚尖翘起，身体重心移至右腿；眼看前方（图 6-171 至图 6-173）。

① Move the left hand forward from under the right wrist and open the right fist. Separate hands and pull them back slowly, palms up, as you sit back with toes of the left foot raised and weight shifted onto the right leg. Look straight ahead (Fig. 6-171 to Fig. 6-173).

图 6-171 (Fig. 6-171)

图 6-172 (Fig. 6-172)

图 6-173 (Fig. 6-173)

② 两手在胸前翻掌,向下经腹前再向上、向前推出,腕部与肩平,手心向前;同时左腿前弓成左弓步;眼看前方(图 6-174 至图 6-176)。

② Turn palms turn over in front of the chest as you pull both hands back to the front of the abdomen and then push them forward and upward until wrists are at shoulder level with palms facing forward. At the same time, bend the left leg for a left bow stance. Look straight ahead (Fig. 6-174 to Fig. 6-176).

图 6-174 (Fig. 6-174)

图 6-175 (Fig. 6-175)

图 6-176 (Fig. 6-176)

要点:身体后坐时,避免后仰,臀部不可凸出。两臂随身体回收时,肩、肘部

Points to Remember: Do not lean backward or protrude buttocks when sitting back. Do not pull arms

略向外松开，不要直着抽回。两手推出宽度不要超过两肩。

back straight. Relax your shoulders and turn elbows a bit outward. Hands should be no farther than shoulder-width apart when you push them forward.

二三 十字手

① 屈膝后坐，身体重心移向右腿，左脚尖里扣，向右转体；右手随着转体动作向右平摆划弧，与左手成两臂侧平举，掌心向前，肘部微屈；同时右脚尖随着转体稍向外撇，成右侧弓步；眼看右手（图6-177、图6-178）。

23　Crossing hands

① Bend the right knee, sit back and shift weight onto the right leg, which is bent at the knee. Turn the body to the right with toes of the left foot turned inward. Following the body turning, move both hands sideways in a horizontal curve at shoulder level with palms facing forward and elbows slightly bent. Meanwhile, turn toes of the right foot slightly outward for a right side bow stance. Look at the right hand (Fig. 6-177, Fig. 6-178).

图 6-177　(Fig. 6-177)

图 6-178　(Fig. 6-178)

图 6-179　(Fig. 6-179)

② 身体重心慢慢移至左腿，右脚尖里扣，随即向左收回，两脚距离与肩同宽，两腿逐渐蹬直，成开立步，同时两手向下经腹前向上划弧交叉合抱于胸前，两臂撑圆，腕高与肩平，右手在外，成十字手，手心均向后；眼看前方（图6-179、图6-180）。

② Shift weight slowly onto the left leg with toes of the right foot turned inward. Then bring the right foot towards the left foot so that they are parallel to each other and shoulder-width apart; straighten legs gradually. At the same time, move both hands down in a vertical curve to cross them. At first, the wrists are in front of the abdomen and then in front of the chest with the left hand nearer to the body and both palms facing inward. Look straight ahead (Fig. 6-179, Fig. 6-180).

要点：两手分开和合抱时，上体不要前俯。站起后，身体自然正直，头要微向上顶，下颏稍向后收。两臂环抱时须圆满舒适，沉肩垂肘。

Points to Remember: Do not lean forward when separating or crossing hands. When taking the parallel stance, keep the body and head erect with chin tucked slightly inward. Keep arms rounded in a comfortable position with shoulders and elbows held down.

二四　收势

① 两手交叉缓缓向前掤出，两臂内旋，两手反转分开，手心向下平举于身前，与肩同宽同高，目视正前方（图6-181）。

② 两臂徐徐下落至大腿外侧，成起势前状，左脚轻轻收回，与右脚并拢，与预备式相同（图6-182、图6-183）。

24　Closing

① The crossed-arms push slowly forward and rotate inward. Turn over both hands to face downward and separate them in front of the body at the shoulders' width and height. Look straight ahead（Fig. 6-181）.

② Drop the arms slowly to the sides of the body, similar to the opening form. Bring the foot gently back next to the right foot. This is the same as the "Preparing" position（Fig. 6-182，Fig. 6-183）.

图 6-180　(Fig. 6-180)　　图 6-181　(Fig. 6-181)　　图 6-182　(Fig. 6-182)　　图 6-183　(Fig. 6-183)

要点：两手左右分开下落时，要注意全身放松，同时气也徐徐下沉（呼气略加长）。呼吸平稳后，把左脚收到右脚旁，再走动休息。

Points to Remember: Keep the whole body relaxed and draw a deep breath（exhalation to be somewhat prolonged）when your hands separate down. Bring the left foot close to the right foot after your breath is even. Walk about for complete recovery.

24式太极拳全套演练

参考文献
References

［1］全国体育院校教材委员会.中国武术教程［M］.北京：人民体育出版社，2002.
［2］陈正雷.陈氏太极拳术［M］.山西：山西科学技术出版社，1999.
［3］李茹彬，董华龙.大学体育实践教程［M］.山东：中国海洋大学出版社，2012.
［4］国家体育总局健身气功管理中心.健身气功［M］.北京：人民体育出版社，2007.
［5］杨文轩，陈琦.体育原理［M］.北京：高等教育出版社，2004.
［6］王言群.新编健身气功的理论构建［M］.北京：北京体育大学出版社，2009.
［7］刘静.太极拳健身理论论绎［M］.北京：北京体育大学出版社，2008.
［8］冀运希.健身气功［M］.北京：人民教育出版社，2007.
［9］温搏.太极拳中英双语教程［M］.北京：北京师范大学出版社，2014.
［10］李颖.健身气功·五禽戏［M］.辽宁：大连海事大学出版社，2016.